English Frameworking

The creative literacy course for English at 11–14

2

Julia Strong
Deputy Director, National Literacy Trust
Pam Bloomfield
Emily Rought-Brooks

National Literacy Trust
Building a literate nation

Published by HarperCollins*Publishers* Limited
77–85 Fulham Palace Road
Hammersmith
London
W6 8JB

www.**Collins**Education.com
On-line support for schools and colleges

British Library Cataloguing in Publication Data
A catalogue record for this publication is available from the
British Library.

Acknowledgements

The publishers gratefully acknowledge the following for
permission to reproduce copyright material.

Text: Dear John letters from *Collins School Grammar* by John
Mannion, published by Collins Educational. Reprinted by
permission of HarperCollins Publishers, p8; extract from
Cider with Rosie by Laurie Lee, published by Hogarth Press.
Used by permission of The Random House Group Limited,
p9; extract from 'The Woollen Bank Forgeries' by Keith
Waterhouse, published by Penguin Books. Reprinted by
permission of David Higham Associates Limited, p13; extract
'Thrilla in Rhyla' from *The Sun*, 17 May 2001. Copyright ©
Times Newspapers Limited, 17 May 2001. Reprinted with
permission, p15; extract from *Northern Lights* by Philip
Pullman, published by Scholastic Limited, p18; extracts from
Heaven Eyes by David Almond, published by Hodder &
Stoughton Limited. Reprinted by permission of the
publishers, pp20, 25; extracts from *My Family and Other
Animals* by Gerald Durrell. Reproduced with permission of
Curtis Brown Ltd, London, on behalf of the Estate of Gerald
Durrell. Copyright Gerald Durrell, pp22, 33; extract from *Life
on Earth* by David Attenborough, published by HarperCollins
Publishers. Reprinted by permission of HarperCollins
Publishers, p31; extract from The Globe Theatre Website.
Reprinted by permission of International Shakespeare Globe
Centre Limited, p53; extracts from *The Undiscovered
Cotswolds: Official Visitors Guide 2001* published by Advance
Publications. Reprinted with permission, p57; extract from
Shakespeare Country Holiday: Short Breaks Guide produced by
South Warwickshire Tourism. Reprinted with permission,
p59; 'Listen Mr Oxford Don' by John Agard. Copyright ©
John Agard. Reprinted by permission of the author and
Caroline Sheldon Literary Agency, p63; 'City Friends Advice'
and 'The Wise Old Timer' by Benjamin Zephaniah, from
School's Out published by AK Press. Copyright © Benjamin
Zephaniah. Reprinted with permission of the author, pp65,
67; 'Advice to a Teenage Daughter' from *Ultrasonics of Snow*
by Isobel Thrilling published by Rivelin-grapheme. Copyright
© Isobel Thrilling. Reprinted with permission of the author,
p65; 'Midsummer Tobago' from *Sea Grapes* by Derek Walcott,
published by Jonathan Cape. Used by permission of The
Random House Group Limited, p68; extracts from *Tales Alive
in Turkey* by Warren Walker and Ahmet E. Uysal, published
by Texas Tech University. Reprinted by permission of Warren
Walker, pp90, 91; review by Shazma Zaman aged 14 of
Nightjohn by Gary Paulsen, from issue no. 1 of Well Worth
Reading's *Boox* reading promotion. Reprinted by permission
of the publishers, p92; front page from *The Mirror*, 2 May

2001. Reprinted by permission of The Mirror Group, p96;
front page from *The Independent*, 2 May 2001, authors Steve
Boggan, Jason Bennetto, Cahal Milmo and Matthew Beard.
Reprinted by permission of The Independent/Syndication,
p96; front page from *The Times*, 24 January 1951. Copyright
© Times Newspapers Limited, 24 January 1951. Reprinted
with permission of Times Newspapers Limited/Syndication,
p96; extract from *You Made Me* (*Collins Plays Plus*) by Kelvin
Reynolds and Adrian Lockwood, published by HarperCollins
Publishers. Reprinted by permission of HarperCollins
Publishers, p110; extract 'Graffiti King' by Linda Hawkins,
from *NOW* magazine, 30 May 2001. Copyright © Linda
Hawkins/Now/IPC Syndication. Reprinted with permission of
IPC Syndication, p133.

Photos: P.J. Arkle, p5; Bubbles, pp5, 135; Corbis Images, pp5,
31, 39; Penguin Books Ltd, p9; Mary Evans Picture Library,
pp 10, 39, 40, 43, 49, 83, 87; PA photos, pp26, 83, 94, 114;
© Nicholas Mander, pp39, 57; John Walmsley, pp 47, 105;
Nigel Jordan, p53; Shakespeare Birthplace Trust, p59; BBC,
p61; Steve Hall, p61; Hulton Archive, pp61, 73, 77, 78;
Photonica, pp65, 67; The Mirror, pp83, 96; Timepix, p84; BFI
Stills, Posters and Designs, p89; Macmillan Publishers for the
cover of *Nightjohn* by Gary Paulsen, p92; © The British
Library, p96; The Independent, p96; Terry Austin-Smith,
pp121, 125; The Coca-Cola Company, p133; Christopher
Srnka, p145.

Cover and internal design by Ken Vail Graphic Design

Commissioned by Helen Clark

Edited by Rachel Orme-Smith and Kim Richardson

The publishers would like to thank Rachel Orme-Smith
for her outstanding editorial contribution to
English Frameworking.

Production by Katie Morris

Printed and bound by Scotprint, UK

Whilst every effort has been made both to contact the
copyright holders and to give exact credit lines, this has not
proved possible in every case.

Internal artwork by Martin Orme, p17; Felicity House, p22;
Zhenya Matysiak, pp26-7, 143, 148, 149; Sarah Warburton,
p28; Ken Vail Graphic Design, pp83, 99; Paul McCaffrey,
p91; Jeff Anderson, p115.

NLT website
www.literacytrust.org.uk

Contents and skills matching grid

Section	Page	Word level	Sentence level	Text level Reading	Text level Writing	Speaking and listening
				(Learning objectives*)		
Reviewing Year 7	5	1, 2, **6a**, 8	**1**, 2, 3, 14		4, 6	**10**
Imagine, explore, entertain	17	1d, 11		4, **5**, 7, **10–13**	3, **5–8**	**1**, 3, 9, **10**
Post-1914 novel	18					
Literary non-fiction (the natural world)	30					
Inform, explain, describe	39	1e, 3, 14	**1, 6**, 9, **10**, 12, 13	1, **2–4**, 6, 9, 15	10, **11**, 12	**1**, 6, 9, 12
Starting Shakespeare (plays, reference and information texts)	40					
Information and reference texts (CD-ROMs, brochures)	52					
Persuade, argue, advise	61	**4, 6b, 6g**, 7a, 11, 13	2, 7, 9	4, 6, 7, **10**, 14, 16	9, 13, **14**, 15	
Post-1914 poetry (including poetry from different cultures and traditions)	62					
Literary non-fiction (reportage)	72					
Analyse, review, comment	83	**4**, 5, **6c–f**, 7b, **10**	5, **11**	3–**5**, 8–**10**, **13**	1, **16–18**	**1, 2**, 4–**7**, 8, 9, 11
Pre-1914 short stories	84					
Media texts (moving image, newspapers, websites)	94					
Plan, draft, present	105	5, **6a**, 7c, 9, 12	4, 8, **10**, **11**	4, **10, 13**	1, **2–4**	**1**, 3, 9, 12–**16**
Recent and contemporary drama	106					
Formal presentations and reports	116					
Pulling it all together	127					
Preparing for NCTs	139					
Reading and the tests	140					
Writing and the tests	146					
Glossary	151					

ey objectives are in bold

Introduction

English Frameworking has been written to make English accessible to all.

By the beginning of your second year in secondary school you should be becoming a confident reader and writer, capable of identifying the purpose, audience and form of any piece of text or any writing task, and thus able to structure and express your ideas coherently both when speaking and writing.

This year you'll be developing your reading, writing and speaking and listening skills, focusing on a wide range of interesting areas. You'll start by analysing and discussing the key differences between English and any other languages that you know. You'll be using the internet to help you research what Shakespeare's contemporaries thought about witches and presenting your findings as a leaflet.

You'll be looking at how poets from different cultures and traditions have expressed their ideas, and have a go at expressing your own ideas. There'll be a range of practical activities to build up your skills in spelling, punctuation and crafting sentences, as well as help with how to structure, draft and refine your work.

Throughout, there's a focus on developing your enjoyment of reading. A wide range of novels, short stories and other texts are introduced to you, and you are asked to focus on your own reading. You'll be looking at how storytellers tell stories, and constructing effective stories of your own.

You'll be considering how modern methods of communication are changing our expectations about news, by looking at how news is presented in newspapers, on television and on the internet. And you'll be analysing how different papers present the same controversial news item and presenting a balanced overview of your analysis.

You'll also be looking at extracts from plays written by modern playwrights, and learn more about the craft of effective script writing. Then you're going to improvise, script and perform your own short scenes.

You'll be rounding off the year not just with a focus on what you need to do to succeed in National Curriculum Tests but by making a class magazine that will pull together all the skills that you have developed over the year and provide you with a publishing opportunity.

Most of all, you'll be joining in a wide range of entertaining and challenging activities which will help you develop your English skills, so that you can succeed in English and in all subjects across the curriculum.

Introduction

To begin this year, you are going to pull together all the work that you did last year, while focusing on the language that helps you talk about language. You're going to start off thinking about what other languages you may know or have recently started learning, apart from English, and analyse the key differences between these languages and English. Then you'll be drawing on all your knowledge about punctuation and discussing how it helps writers express ideas clearly while helping readers understand what is intended. After that, you'll look at figurative imagery and at the sentence structures that help you write effectively in all genres. You'll also be thinking about how to develop your spelling skills. To pull everything together, you are going to play a game that tests your ability to express your knowledge and understanding of text, grammar and punctuation. You'll then be in a good position to develop all your reading, writing and speaking and listening skills in English – as well as in your other lessons.

Key aim

In this section you will:

- Build on your knowledge and understanding of the language of language and how to write effectively.

Aims

On these two pages you will:

- Use your knowledge of other languages to identify differences and similarities with the English language.
- Use key terms that help to describe and analyse language.
- Use talk to develop your understanding of complex issues.

Starter
as a class

If you're lucky enough to know another language apart from English, you'll already know how much this can help you understand about the nature of language. You're going to start this year by finding out how many different languages are known by members of your class.

Your teacher is going to write on the board:

You can see that:

- The subject of the sentence, the noun 'cat', has been underlined.
- The adjective, 'black', has a line above it.
- The verb, 'sat', has been circled.
- The adverbial phrase, 'on the mat', has a squiggly line under it.

Your teacher will be asking for volunteers to write this sentence up in as many different languages as members of the class speak. When you have written the sentence in the language that you know, work out which words are the subject 'cat', the verb 'sat', the adjective 'black' and

the adverbial phrase 'on the mat'. Indicate them in the same way as in the example.

As the different versions are put on the board, discuss the different word orders that start to appear.

English:

The black cat (sat) on the mat.

French:

Le chat noir (s'est assis) sur le tapis.

Turkish:

Kara kedi kilimin üstünde (oturdu.)

Introduction
as a class

Listen carefully while your teacher read you an extract from *Mother Tongue*, a book by Bill Bryson which tells the sto of the English language (**Worksheet 1**) Discuss this as a class, focusing on the following questions:

1 What are the advantages and disadvantages of English having so many different words that mean almost the same thing? (Paragraph

2 Why do you think some languages have specialist words which don't ex in other languages? (Paragraphs 2–3)

3 What does the writer mean when h describes the English language as very flexible? What are the advantages and disadvantages of this? (Paragraph 4)

Bill Bryson is an American journalist and writer who is best known for his amusing travel books – the one on the British Isles is called *Notes from a Small Island*. He has also written a range of books on grammar and the nature of the English language.

Development *as a group*

Your teacher will divide you into groups of two to four so that people who know the same language are working together. Your task is to construct a sentence in the language you are focusing on that brings out some key differences between that language and English. Then annotate that sentence to explain the differences and similarities. Think about the following points:

- **Word order** – see the starter activity.
- **Joining words together** – are some words joined together to make one long word?
- **Word endings** – do words change their spelling to indicate different tenses, person etc?
- **Pronunciation** – is there a complete match between the way the language is written and the way it is pronounced?
- **Gender** – do nouns and adjectives have masculine, feminine and neuter forms?
- **Alphabet** – is the Roman alphabet used (the one used in English)?

Be prepared to present your sentence to the class (each member of the group should present a different aspect). Look at how some students annotated a Turkish sentence (below).

Plenary

Listen and watch carefully while the groups present their points to the class. Be prepared to ask questions about other groups' presentations, especially if you don't understand what points they are making. Try to use the correct grammatical terms when you speak.

Comparing Turkish and English

1 Word order is completely different	2 Consistent pronunciation based on pronouncing every syllable

Dün sokaktaki gördügümüz kedi hastaymış. (5 words)

3 Joining together of words	4 Alphabet very similar to Roman alphabet, but some letters different

Apparently, the cat that we saw on the street yesterday is ill. (12 words)
Yesterday street at which saw that we cat is ill apparently. (Literal translation)

Why bother with punctuation?

Aims

On these two pages you will:

- Think about how punctuation and paragraphs help you understand text.
- Review the functions of all the different punctuation marks and write sentences to illustrate some of them.
- Use talk to develop your understanding of complex issues.

Starter  on your own

Read both of the texts below to yourself carefully.

Dear John,

I want a man who knows what love is all about. You are generous, kind, thoughtful. People who are not like you admit to being useless and inferior. You have ruined me for other men. I yearn for you. I have no feelings whatsoever when we're apart. I can be forever happy – will you let me be yours?

Gloria

Dear John,

I want a man who knows what love is. All about you are generous, kind, thoughtful people, who are not like you. Admit to being useless and inferior. You have ruined me. For other men, I yearn. For you, I have no feelings whatsoever. When we're apart, I can be forever happy. Will you let me be?

Yours,

Gloria

Be prepared to read each text out loud to the class, using the punctuation to bring out the intended meaning.

What difference does the punctuation make?

Introduction as a group

Your teacher will give you a copy of the opening paragraphs of Laurie Lee's autobiography *Cider with Rosie* (**Worksheet 2**). The trouble is, all the punctuation marks and paragraphs have been removed. In groups, read it out loud to each other and see if you can decide how it should be read. Mark the punctuation and paragraphs on a copy of the text to help you in this reading. (You will also have to turn some letters into capital letters.)

Laurie Lee has included at least one example of all the punctuation marks displayed on page 9. Make certain you have included all of these when you mark up your text.

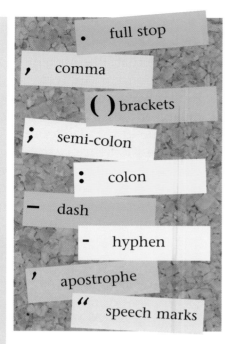

- full stop
- , comma
- ( ) brackets
- ; semi-colon
- : colon
- — dash
- - hyphen
- ' apostrophe
- " speech marks

Be prepared to be asked to read your interpretation to the class or to show the class how you have punctuated the piece.

- What difference does punctuation make to the passage?
- What difference do paragraphs make?

Development *as a group*

1 Each punctuation mark serves a purpose. Your teacher will give you cards with all the different punctuation marks, and cards that describe their function (**Worksheet** 3). In groups, your task is to match each punctuation mark with the card or cards that describe its function. (Some marks have only one function card; others have up to three.) Be prepared to feed back your ideas to the class.

2 See if you can find an example of each type of punctuation in the opening of *Cider with Rosie*. Write the number of the card against each punctuation mark in the extract on **Worksheet 4**. Here is the first sentence to start you off:

2 **10**

I was set down from the carrier's cart at the age of three; and there with a sense of bewilderment and terror my life in the village began.

1

Laurie Lee (1914–1997) is a British poet and writer, best known for *Cider with Rosie* (1959), his autobiographical account of his early life in a remote Cotswold village.

Plenary

On your whiteboard, or on a piece of paper, jot down two reasons why punctuation is important.

homework

Which punctuation functions are *not* illustrated in the extract from *Cider with Rosie*? For homework, construct sentences of your own to illustrate each of these functions.

Painting pictures with words

Aims

On these two pages you will:

- Analyse how Laurie Lee has used figurative language to make a scene vivid.
- Create a sense of character and setting by using figurative language.
- Explore the impact of a variety of sentence structures.

Starter  in pairs

Last lesson you used your knowledge of punctuation to punctuate the opening paragraphs of *Cider with Rosie*. Now you are going to use your knowledge of figurative language to focus on what makes it such an effective piece of writing.

Read the extract again on **Worksheet 4** (the figurative imagery has been highlighted).

- Label each example of figurative language – is it a simile, a metaphor or personification?
- Put a squiggly line under any description in the passage that helps you picture how small Laurie Lee was when this story took place and how large things seemed to him.
- Underline the images that you think are the most effective.
- Put an asterisk against any short simple sentences.

Here is an example of how you might annotate the passage:

metaphor

It towered above me and all around me, each blade tattooed with tiger-skins of sunlight.

metaphor

Be prepared to present your analysis to the class.

Introduction on your own

Imagine that, like Alice in Wonderland or Gulliver, suddenly you have shrunk to a height of only a few inches. You are alone in the classroom. Imagine what the classroom would look like if you were only that height and how big it would seem. Think about the emotions you would be going through.

You are going to describe this experience in a piece of writing. What images would help to recreate the scene and your feelings so that a reader could picture it? You may find it useful to bend down and see what the classroom looks like from six inches above the ground. What images best describe all the chair and table legs that are now all around you? Does the gap between the tables now look more like an avenue than an aisle? Use your whiteboard or a piece of paper to jot down some images. Ensure that you have a mix of metaphors and similes and, if possible, some personification.

You might want to develop some of the following ideas:

Desks and table legs

tower

glower

mock

crowd

look down

forest

Size

mouse-like

cat's-eye view

- Decide whether you want to write your piece in the past tense or in the present tense.
- Try to mix short simple sentences and longer figurative descriptive sentences, as Laurie Lee does.

Development *on your own*

Now draft your description. Aim at writing a few effective descriptive paragraphs rather than attempting to write a story.

When you have completed your first draft, read it through carefully and rework your sentences, making them as effective as possible. Remember to use:

- Variety of sentence length
- Repetition for effect
- Figurative language
- Powerful verbs.

Plenary

In groups of four, read each others' descriptions and decide which is the best of the four. Decide who is going to read the description to the class.

Listen while the selected descriptions are read to the class. Discuss which images are the most effective and what makes them so powerful.

homework

For homework, redraft your description in the light of the class's discussion, so that it is even more effective. Put an asterisk in the margin against the lines you think are the most effective.

> ! **Remember** to read your description through carefully, correcting any mistakes. Write a comment at the bottom telling your teacher how well you think you have done this piece of work.

Last year you read a wide range of books. In the next section you will be focusing on reading. If you liked the extract from *Cider with Rosie* you may be interested in reading the whole book to find out the full story of Laurie Lee's childhood. Or you may prefer *As I Walked out One Midsummer Morning*, which tells the story of his walk across Spain as a young man on the eve of civil war. Keith Waterhouse, the writer of 'The Woollen Bank Forgeries' which you will read on page 13, is well known as a television script writer; he is also the author of the very entertaining novel *Billy Liar* about a young man who is incapable of telling the truth.

Crafting effective sentences

Aims

On these two pages you will:

- Review compound and complex sentences.
- Develop your understanding of subordinate clauses.
- Think about what factors make handwriting easy to read, and set yourself targets to improve your own handwriting.

Starter  as a class

Look at the handwriting below.

> Please write a note and leave it for me next to the fridge

Which words are particularly difficult to read? Can you work out why?

> **! Remember**
>
> - If you misjoin your letters, it can make your writing very hard to read. It also can make words appear to have been misspelt.
> - Only 'w', 'v', 'o', 'f' and 'r' join at the top.

 in pairs

Swap your writing book with your partner's and look at the handwriting. Fill in the grid on **Worksheet 5** to help you analyse your partner's writing. Then discuss your conclusions with your partner before setting your own handwriting targets.

Introduction

Good writers can control sentences effectively. Often this means combining clauses in different ways. The two clauses in the example below are main clauses because either can stand on its own and make complete sense. In these sentences (called **compound sentences**) the clauses are joined with conjunctions such as 'and' and 'but'.

> Main clause

Richard went to the cinema but Ruth went bowling.

> Main clause joined to first main clause with conjunction 'but'

Sometimes, though, you want to give more information about the main clause. This creates **complex sentences**, which consist of one main clause and one or more **subordinate clauses**. The subordinate clauses, which do not make sense if they stand alone, are joined to the main clause by **subordinating conjunctions**. These conjunctions help the reader or listener to understand the relationship between one part of a sentence and another. In the example below, 'while' shows that both activities happened at the same time:

> Main clause

Richard went to the cinema while Ruth went bowling.

> Subordinate clause joined to main clau with subordinating conjunction 'while

Listen carefully to the pattern of the language when your teacher reads you the opening paragraphs of 'The Woollen Bank Forgeries'. Think about how the writer, Keith Waterhouse, has used subordinate clauses in the extract. Decide what are the answers to the questions at the side of the passage and be prepared to discuss your ideas with the class.

his a npound or mplex tence? w do you w?

ere is the n clause in sentence? ntify the

ordinate ses, ether n their ordinating junctions

at is the nection ween the two ses in this ence? at ctuation s to post the ordinate se?

at is the n clause his ence? y many s are e to this ence?

When I was nine years old, I developed an insane passion for a cricket set on Woolworth's toy counter. This was in the days when everything at Woollie's cost either threepence or sixpence. Sixpence for the bat, ball sixpence, stumps sixpence, bails threepence, pads sixpence apiece, analysis book threepence, total three shillings. I made up my mind that I was going to have the cricket set. **Long before I worked out how I was going to steal the money, I was rehearsing what I would say to my mother when I took the gear home for the first time.**

"No, only they've started a cricket team in our class. And do you know who's got to look after all the stuff, mam? Me."

Immediate suspicion. "How do you mean, you've got to look after it? Why can't they look after their own stuff?"

"Ah well, it's not really a school team, it's just our teacher. Old Webby. Mr Webb. **He sees us all playing cricket in the street with an old tennis ball, so he says we could start our own team up in that field,** and all look after the stuff in turns. He said we shouldn't be playing in the street."

"Yes, and I've told you not to play in the street as well."

My mother, with her flat damp voice, was so predictable that I could make up whole conversations with her before I got into the house, examining and re-examining every statement for flaws, leading myself up my own garden path and <u>reconnoitring</u>[1] for trip-wires.

[1] *looking closely*

complex sentence a sentence containing one main clause and one or more subordinate clauses

compound sentence a sentence made up of two or more main clauses joined by a conjunction such as 'and' or 'but'

subordinate clause a clause that adds information to the main clause of the sentence

subordinating conjunction a word or phrase such as 'when', 'although', 'before', 'until', 'where', 'like', 'as', 'because', 'since', 'so that', 'in order to' and 'if' which introduces a subordinate clause: 'I spoke to Dad <u>when</u> I got home'

Development

Now it's your turn to write an effective short description of guilt. You may want to make up an incident that happens to someone else or think of a time when you have been expecting to get into trouble for something. Aim at writing a few effective descriptive paragraphs rather than attempting to write a story.

Remember to vary your sentence length and structure so that you include complex and compound sentences, just as Keith Waterhouse has done. You may find some of the following sentence starters useful.

- *Sitting outside the headteacher's office, ...*
- *As soon as she heard her mother's voice, ...*
- *Looking quickly to see that no one was watching, ...*

Plenary

Why is it important to be able to write in complex sentences?

Textopoly!

Aims

On these two pages you will:

- Play a game that reviews much of what you've learnt about text and grammar and the vocabulary that describes it.
- Use talk to develop your understanding of complex issues.
- Review the spelling conventions you focused on last year.

Starter  on your own

Your teacher is going to test you on 20 words that students in your class have had difficulty with recently.

 in pairs

A student in your year has recently misspelled 20 words and entered them in their spelling log. You will be given a copy of these words (**Worksheet 6**) plus some blank pieces of paper on which to add any words that you or your partner have misspelled in the test that you have just been given.

1 Sort the words into the five spelling convention categories that you have been given (these are different aspects of words that may cause difficulty when you spell them):

- Vowel choices
- Plurals
- Word endings
- Prefixes
- **Homophones.**

If a word seems to fit more than one category, place it in the category that you think fits best.

2 What advice can you give the student about how they might be helped to remember these words?

- What spelling patterns emerge?
- Are there related words that may help?
- Would a **mnemonic** be useful?
- Are easily confused words causing a problem?
- Are they checking their work carefully?

 3 Reflect on what advice you would give yourself and add any words that you had difficulty spelling to your spelling log.

homophone a word that sounds the same as another but has a different spelling and meaning: 'right' and 'write'
mnemonic a strategy or method of remembering something: 'There is <u>a rat</u> in separate'

Introduction as a group

Your teacher will give you a pack of question cards so that you can play Textopoly!, the text analysis and grammar game (**Worksheets 7–10**). First you are going to have a trial run, so that you understand exactly how to play. Follow the first six instructions in the rules on page 15 as your teacher explains them to you.

Development as a group

Now it's time to play the game. The winner will have to justify their answers to the whole class at the end of the lesson, so be prepared to explain your answers clearly in formal English.

Appoint a scorer to note down the scores, and then you are ready to begin. The player who started the trial game should now start the actual game.

Plenary

The winning student will explain the answers that they gave to the questions on their cards. See if you agree with the answers given.

Learn any words that you misspelled in today's test, and check that you can now spell all the recent additions to your spelling log.

Textopoly! – the text analysis and grammar game

RULES

1. Shuffle the cards and place them face down in the centre of the group of four players.

2. Toss a coin to see who becomes the first player, then go clockwise.

3. The first player turns over the first card and reads it to the group. If it's a **Knowledge** or **Understanding** card he/she attempts to answer.

4. The rest of the group judge if the answer is good enough to gain marks, and the scorer notes down the score. The answerer places the card in front of them.

5. If the answer is wrong, the question is passed back anti-clockwise round the group until the correct answer is given. If no one knows the answer, no score is given.

6. If the card picked up is a **Text analysis** card, the player reads the card aloud and attempts to analyse what sort of text it is, supporting their answer with at least two reasons relating to the purpose, structure or style of the text. If the player cannot answer, the whole group tries to answer collectively. In this case, each member of the group is awarded one point.

7. The first student in the class to gain 10 points calls out *Textopoly!*

Knowledge question 2 (1 mark)
What is a subordinate clause?

Understanding question 9 (2 marks)
Join the following two sentences together without using 'and', 'but' or 'so' and explain what you have done.
The girl was very late.
The teacher was annoyed.

Text analysis card 5 (up to 4 marks)
Say what sort of text you think this is and point out at least two features that are typical of this sort of text.

THE SUN SAYS

Thrilla in Rhyla

Well, well, well ... who said this election was going to be boring.

New Labour has reached out to the people and the people have fought back – *literally*.

Tony Blair was yelled at Jack St

! *Remember*

- When you have successfully answered a card, lay it face down in front of you.
- The more the group argues unnecessarily, the less chance there will be of anyone in the group being the winner.

Reviewing what's been learnt

In this section you have thought about the differences between English and other languages, and have developed your understanding of the structure of the English language. You should also have increased your understanding of punctuation, figurative language and complex sentences, and have done some writing that demonstrates this.

You now have some targets for improving your handwriting and are aware of which strategies will help you improve your spelling. Finally, you should now feel confident about identifying and discussing the key features of any text type.

Now it's time to think about what things you have learnt from this section, and list the key points in your exercise book, using these sentence starters to help you:

The key things I have learnt about writing in this section are ...

The key things I have learnt about punctuation are ...

The things I have learnt about the differences between the English language and _____ are ...

I now understand more about ...

The words I have learnt to spell are ...

The things I found most difficult were ...

The things I think I did best were ...

I now feel more confident about ...

My targets to improve my work are: (include reading, writing, spelling, speaking and listening)

-
-
-
-
-
-

Imagine, explore, entertain

Introduction

Have you ever thought about the power of the written word? Novels, poems, short stories, drama, fiction or non-fiction – they all have the power to transport you to a different world. Reading can help to feed your imagination, allow you to explore other worlds and keep you entertained, all at the same time.

This section will help you to develop your critical reading skills, which will enable you to make a more informed choice of your own reading material. By the end of the section you may wish to include literary non-fiction as well as recent novels in your reading list.

By exploring different texts and the variety of approaches that authors use, you will also become increasingly aware of literary devices that could be incorporated into your own writing. Developing your skills will help you to explore your own imagination with a more critical focus, allowing you to entertain your readers and listeners alike.

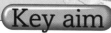

Key aim

In this section you will:

- Analyse and explore the craft of writing, particularly through your own reading, to enable you to develop your own narrative and descriptive style.

What do you read?

Aims

On these two pages you will:

- Talk in groups to discuss and develop your ideas about reading.
- Study the style and content of extracts from different books.
- Begin some independent reading of your own.

Starter as a group

In groups of four, discuss these questions:

1 Why is reading important?

2 What do you enjoy reading?

Make a list of all the factors that you take into consideration when choosing a book to read (for example, length, author, cover, topic …). Then put these factors into an agreed order of importance. Be ready to feed back to the class when your time is up.

Introduction

Almost everyone enjoys reading. You have only to look at people on tubes and trains, or waiting for the dentist, and you will see them reading. Once we have acquired this priceless skill, we never forget it. We read because we like to explore the world beyond ourselves.

as a class

In groups of four, read and think about the extract below. Then discuss these questions:

1 What type of writing would you say this was? How do you know? Give three reasons for your answer, using quotations where appropriate.

2 Which aspects of this extract do you like or dislike? Support your view by giving examples from the text.

> Philip Pullman (born 1946) has won many literary awards for his children's writing. He has just completed the trilogy *His Dark Materials*.

Lyra had an impression of blood-stained muzzle[1] and face, small malevolent[2] black eyes, and an immensity of dirty matted yellowish fur. As it gnawed, hideous growling, crunching, sucking noises came from it.

The bear stopped eating. As far as they could tell, he was looking at them directly, but it was impossible to read any expression on his face.

Lyra's heart was thumping hard, because something in the bear's presence made her feel close to coldness, danger, brutal power, but a power controlled by intelligence; and not a human intelligence, nothing like a human, because of course bears had no daemons.[3]

This strange hulking presence gnawing its meat was like nothing she had ever imagined, and she felt a profound admiration and pity for the lonely creature.

He dropped the reindeer leg in the dirt and slumped on all fours to the gate. Then he reared up massively, ten feet or more high, as if to show how mighty he was, to remind them how useless the gate would be as a barrier, and he spoke to them from that height.

'Well? Who are you?'

His voice was so deep it seemed to shake the earth. The rank[4] smell that came from his body was almost overpowering.

[1] *nose and mouth*
[2] *evil, wanting to cause harm*
[3] *guardian spirits*
[4] *offensive, unpleasant*

on your own

Think about how the author has engaged your interest in this passage. Apart from making the setting, characters and action in their stories exciting, authors also use techniques to ensure that their writing is stimulating for the reader. For example, they may:

- Use imaginative vocabulary, such as powerful verbs and adjectives, to create an atmosphere. (For example, they may use 'bellowed' instead of 'said'.)
- Use sentences that vary in length and structure.
- Create an atmosphere of tension, mystery or fear.

What evidence can you find in this extract that the author uses any of these techniques?

Be ready to feed back to the class, quoting directly from the extract to support your ideas.

Development **as a group**

Each group of four will be given an extract to study (**Worksheets 11a–b**). Assess the writing, using the same criteria as you used in the introduction activity, both in the class discussion and on your own.

You will then be asked to form different groups, where you as the 'expert' on your particular extract will be asked to feed back your conclusions to your new group.

After you have had feedback on all the extracts, as a group decide which extract you like the most and why.

(Of course it is not always possible to tell whether you are going to like reading a book just by reading one short extract, but extracts do give you an idea about the writer's style and narrative skill.)

Plenary

Write on your whiteboard, or on a piece of paper, the three most important factors that influence you when you choose a book to read.

Independent reading

While you are working through this section, your teacher will ask you to read a novel on your own. Use the information you have been gathering in this lesson to help you choose something that you will find interesting.

In this section you will be learning more about the craft of writing, which will help you to appreciate further the techniques that writers use. Apply your learning to the book you are reading and record your responses on the first part of **Worksheet 12**. At the end of this section you will be asked to give a short presentation on one of the books you have read.

Make sure that you:

- Record your responses on **Worksheet 12**.
- Choose a book that will interest you, and perhaps stretch and challenge you.
- Choose something that you might not ordinarily read.
- Start reading it immediately – it has to be finished by the end of the section.
- Read more than one book if you can.

19

Engaging the reader's interest

Aims

On these two pages you will:

- Investigate texts to see how the author engages the interest of the reader.
- Understand the importance of narrative perspective.

Starter

In order to be successful a writer must first capture the interest of potential readers, making sure that they will want to read the rest of the story.

The extract below, which is from the very beginning of David Almond's novel *Heaven Eyes*, demonstrates some of the techniques that authors use.

One technique is to address the reader directly. For example, he tells us, 'You'll know her easily' (line 9). Later he almost gives us an order: 'Listen to her strange sweet voice' (line 10), as if we were there with the character herself.

Another technique is to hint at the story that follows: 'We did see Grampa return to the river' (line 6), or to offer a comment on it: 'But they did happen' (line 4).

in pairs

In pairs, find other examples in the extract where the author grabs the interest of the reader. Use **Worksheet 13** to structure your discussion and record your responses.

as a class

Feed back your answers.

How do you know that the events in the story have already taken place? How effective is this paragraph in terms of drawing readers into the story?

> David Almond said, 'I always wanted to be a writer, though I told very few people until I was "grown up".'
>
> He has now written four novels for children: *Skellig, Kit's Wilderness, Heaven Eyes* and *Secret Heart*. The autobiography of his childhood, *Counting Stars*, tells us about his early life in a coal mining town above the River Tyne, where he lived with his many brothers and sisters. He now lives in Newcastle where he writes for adults and children. He has won many literary awards.

My name is Erin Law. My friends are January Carr and Mouse Gullane. This is the story of what happened when we sailed away from Whitegates that Friday night. Some people will tell you that none of these things happened. They'll say they were just a dream that the three of us shared. **But they did happen**. We did meet Heaven
5 Eyes on the Black Middens. We did dig the saint out of the mud. We did find Grampa's treasures and his secrets. **We did see Grampa return to the river**. And we did bring Heaven Eyes home with us. She lives happily here among us. People will tell you that this is not Heaven Eyes. They'll say she's just another damaged child like ourselves. But she is Heaven Eyes. **You'll know her easily**. Look at her toes and
10 fingers. **Listen to her strange sweet voice**. Watch how she seems to see through all the darkness in the world to the joy that lies beneath. It is her. These things happen. January, Mouse and I were there to see them all. Everything is true. So listen.

Introduction

When a writer starts to write, whether it is fiction or non-fiction, a novel, reportage or a poem, a number of decisions need to be made. One of the most important of these is choosing the **narrative perspective**. The narrative perspective provides the reader with a window through which the world created by the writer can be seen and experienced.

Sometimes an author will choose to tell a story through the 'voice' of one of the characters. This means that the character concerned tells the story directly, in the first person. Consequently the reader experiences everything from the point of view of that person alone.

> **narrative perspective** the point of view from which a story is written

as a class

Look again at the extract from *Heaven Eyes*, and discuss these questions:

1 Who has the author chosen to be the narrator of the story?

2 How do we know this?

3 What are the advantages and disadvantages of telling a story in this way?

In pairs, discuss these questions:

1 How do you think this particular narrative perspective will affect the reader? For example, will it give the reader greater understanding of feelings?

2 In what way would the reader's understanding be different if the author had chosen a different narrative perspective?

Development in pairs

Read the extract from *Heaven Eyes* on **Worksheet 14**. In pairs:

1 Highlight all the first-person pronouns (I, me, my, we, us).

2 Rewrite the first paragraph, changing the narrative voice from first to third person. (You may also need to make changes to a few other words in places.)

3 Discuss what difference this makes to your involvement in the story as a reader.

4 Which version do you think is more effective? Why?

Plenary

Identify three techniques that authors use to engage their audience.

homework

Imagine a frightening or sad moment in your own life. Using the David Almond extract as a model, write an opening paragraph to your story which:

- Speaks to the reader directly.
- Comments on, or hints at, the story that will follow.
- Is written in the first person.

> **Independent reading**
> Record your ideas on narrative perspective and other techniques in the second part of **Worksheet 12**.

Figurative language and setting.

Aims

On these two pages you will:

- Develop your understanding of figurative language.
- Examine how figurative language can be used to convey a setting.
- Use figurative language to create your own setting.

Starter

One way in which imaginative writers entertain their readers is by using **figurative language**. This means using language in an original way, creating comparisons and links between unlikely objects, or giving things human actions or feelings. Authors use figurative language like this to help them create characters and settings.

in pairs

In the extract above from his book *My Family and Other Animals,* the writer Gerald Durrell has used different types of figurative language (highlighted in bold) to create a setting for one of his stories. In pairs:

1 Read the extract. Discuss each instance of figurative language and decide what type it is.

2 Talk about the image (or picture) that is created through the links and comparisons that have been made. Does it help you to see the scene?

3 Record your responses on **Worksheet 15** and be ready to feed back to the class.

figurative language the use of words or expressions in an abstract or imaginative way to create a particular impression or mood. Imagery such as metaphors, similes and personification are examples of figurative language.

The olives seemed weighed down under the weight of their fruit, **smooth drops of green jade** among which **the choirs of cicadas**[1] **zithered**.[2] In the orange groves, among the dark and shiny leaves, **the fruit was starting to glow redly, like a blush spreading up the green, pitted skins**.

Up on the hills, among the dark <u>cypress</u>[3] and heather, **shoals of butterflies danced and twisted like wind-blown confetti**. The grasshoppers and locusts **whirred like clockwork** under my feet, and **flew drunkenly across the heather**, their wings shining in the sun.

[1] *insects*
[2] *made the sound of a zither (a stringed musical instrument)*
[3] *a tree*

Introduction
as a class

David Almond has used figurative language to create the atmosphere for a very different type of setting in his novel *Heaven Eyes*. He makes the place sinister and menacing through the images and vocabulary that he has chosen.

One of the ideas that David Almond explores in his novel is that there is a very thin line between the 'real' world and the world of the spirit, or between what we think of as 'fact' and 'fiction'. He demonstrates this clearly in the passage where Erin, the narrator, is describing the warehouses where they discover Heaven Eyes living with Grampa.

Read this extract from *Heaven Eyes* together as a class (**Worksheet 16**). Notice the way objects like ceilings and dust are personified (given human actions and feelings). For example, 'Dust seethed all around me' makes it seem as if the very particles in the air around Erin are alive and acting against her. The word 'seethed' itself suggests that the dust is about to boil over in anger.

Almond also repeatedly refers to darkness and imagines ghosts or other creatures lurking in the shadows: 'They were creatures that had grown in darkness and desolation, mutant life forms, half-dead and half-alive.' Images like these help him to create a feeling of threat and fear.

in pairs

In pairs, read the extract on **Worksheet 16** again.

1 Underline or highlight all the words that you think create an atmosphere of darkness and evil.

2 Find examples of two different types of figurative language.

3 Write down three words or phrases that you think are used in a particularly unusual or imaginative way.

4 What is the effect of the atmosphere that Almond has created here? How do you think this has been achieved?

Development
on your own

Now you are going to use figurative language to write your own paragraph describing a shadowy forest. Use the grid on **Worksheet 17** to help you.

(Write your paragraph for homework if you run out of time in the lesson.)

! **Remember** to read your work carefully, improve it if necessary, and write a brief comment on how well you think you have completed the task.

Plenary

Read your paragraph to your partner. Does it include figurative language? Talk about suggestions that you could make to improve your work.

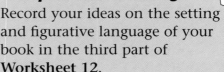

Independent reading

Record your ideas on the setting and figurative language of your book in the third part of **Worksheet 12**.

Structure and theme

Aims

On these two pages you will:

- Study the different ways in which a story can be structured to create different effects.
- Investigate the structure of the novel *Heaven Eyes*.
- Trace the development of themes and ideas in *Heaven Eyes*.

Starter *as a class*

In its simplest form a story can be told in chronological order (the order in which the events occurred). Why do you think an author might choose not to structure a novel in chronological order?

as a group

You are now going to experiment with the effect that an author can create for the reader by choosing to reorder the information given in the recounting of a story.

Each group will be allocated one of the sentences in the box above.

1 Imagine that the sentence you have been given is the starting-point of a re-telling of the Cinderella story.

2 Talk about how you would structure the rest of the story, given this starting-point.

3 Write four or five bullet points, or design a flow chart, to show the new structure of this story.

Feed back your group's findings. Discuss the different effects created by the different structures of the Cinderella story. Which structure works the best?

---

1 'Indeed you shall go to the ball,' announced the fairy godmother to the startled Cinderella.

2 There was a shock in store for Cinderella when one morning her wicked step-mother declared that she would now be working as a servant in her own home.

3 Prince Charming was instantly captivated by the exquisite beauty of the mysterious stranger at the ball.

4 Prince Charming had at last found his own true love.

5 All that was left was a slender silver slipper, and Prince Charming began to search the land for the girl whose foot would fit it.

Introduction

Although an obvious way to tell a story is to start at the beginning and finish at the end, some authors choose to do something different in order to create greater interest or an atmosphere of mystery or suspense. For example, the 19th-century writer Emily Brontë started her novel *Wuthering Heights* in the middle of the story, before returning to the beginning.

In David Almond's novel *Heaven Eyes* the narrator begins by outlining the events of the story that he is about to tell. (Look again at the opening paragraph of the novel on page 20.)

 in pairs

In pairs, investigate the structure of the story of David Almond's novel *Heaven Eyes*.

1 Arrange the story outline boxes (**Worksheet 18**) in what you think is chronological order.

2 Compare your order with that of another pair.

3 Agree on a final order between you.

Development *as a class*

Apart from the structure of the storyline, a writer also needs to consider the way in which the story is told and the **themes** that arise. Some authors have very definite 'trade marks' of style and theme, which combine to create their distinctive 'voice'. If an author's voice appeals to you, you will probably want to read more books by that author.

David Almond is a writer whose work can be clearly identified in this way. As discussed on page 23, a theme running through his novels is how the world of the spirit is all about us. In *Heaven Eyes* this theme is introduced early on in the story.

As a class, read the extract above. Erin, the narrator, is speaking about how she feels that her mother comes back to comfort her, although she is dead.

theme the subject or underlying idea of a piece of writing, for example the triumph of good over evil, or how the world of the spirit is closer to the real world than we think

Yes, I know about pain and darkness. Sometimes I go so far into the darkness that I'm scared I'll not get out again. But I do get out, and I do begin to burn again. I don't need to imagine my life. I don't need the stupid circle times. I don't need to build a stupid Life Story book. My head is filled with memories, is always filled with memories. I see my Mum and me in our little house in St Gabriel's Estate. I feel her touch on my skin. I feel her breath on my face. I smell her perfume. I hear her whispering in my ear. I have my little cardboard treasure box, and at any moment I can bring my lovely Mum back to me.

in pairs

The theme of the spirit world and of the protection and guidance that Erin's mother gives her daughter is further developed throughout the novel. In pairs:

1 Read the series of short extracts from *Heaven Eyes* on **Worksheet 19**.

2 Highlight the references to the spirit world and Erin's mother in each extract.

3 Discuss the differences and similarities in the way in which the theme is introduced in each extract.

4 Do you think that by having this theme running through his novel David Almond is giving his readers a message of some kind? If so, discuss together what this might be.

5 Examine the extracts again to see if you can find any other themes that they may contain.

Plenary

Discuss these questions as a class:

- Why is the structure of a story important?
- What is the difference between the theme of a story and its storyline?

Independent reading

Record your ideas on the structure and themes of your book in the fourth part of **Worksheet 12**.

The magic of writing

Aims

On these two pages you will:

- Review what you have learnt about writing strategies.
- Plan and write a story of your own which engages the interest of your readers.

Starter `as a group`

David Almond says, 'Writing can be difficult, but sometimes it really does feel like a kind of magic. I think that stories are living things – among the most important things in the world.'

He believes that young people should be given the chance to think and explore for themselves, to blur the lines between dreams and reality, to 'be amazed by the world'.

In this lesson you are going to create your own piece of magic by writing a story. To help you, first you must review what you have learnt so far in this section. In groups of four, draw up a checklist to remind you of strategies that you can use in your writing to engage the interest of your readers. For example:

- Addressing the reader directly.
- Using figurative language.
- Structuring your story in an interesting way.

Now feed back your checklist to the class. Add anything to your list that you may have left out.

Introduction `on your own`

Plan a story which has the following storyline:

1. You have been caught in some kind of trap. (You don't have to be human.)
2. You seem to recognize your surroundings, but you are not sure where you are, how you got there or how to get out.
3. At last you free yourself.

Use **Worksheet 20** to help you plan your story. (Remember the checklist you made earlier.)

Now write a draft of the first paragraph or two of your story.

> **! Hints**
>
> - Write in the first person.
> - Structure your story in the order that you think will create the most appropriate effect.
> - Engage the interest of your readers by addressing them directly.
> - Use figurative language in your description.

Development *in pairs*

1 Working in role as a **critical reader**, review the work on your story that each of you has done so far.

2 Help each other to check off the writing strategies that you have used.

3 Highlight three things that you find interesting as a reader and two things that you think could be improved. (Provide some helpful suggestions.)

4 Feed back to your partner and talk about how each of you could continue your stories.

critical reader someone who reads a text in an active and critical way, searching for meaning and looking at what is both good and bad

Plenary

Your teacher will ask some of you to read out your draft of the story so far. Discuss what writing strategies have been used, and how effective they are.

homework

Complete a final draft of your story for homework.

! **Remember** to read your work through carefully, improving it where you think it is necessary. Keep asking yourself, 'How will this interest my reader?' Check that your handwriting and spelling are the very best you can do.

Independent reading

Don't forget to keep up with your independent reading while working through the rest of this section. You will be asked to review this at the end of the section (pages 36–37).

Aims

On these two pages you will:

- Read an ancient and a modern fable.
- Analyse the structure, content and pattern of language used in fables.
- Use what you have learnt to write your own fable.

Starter

You have focused your attention so far on modern novels. Today, however, you will be exploring **fables**. Fables tend to be written using slightly old-fashioned language, and in a simple style, rather like a fairy tale. They often follow this structure:

- **An introduction** – everything is good and wonderful.
- **A complication** – people begin to behave badly.
- **A resolution** – people are punished for what they have done wrong. This often leads to the 'moral' of the tale (a short moral lesson at the end).

as a group

Read the fable 'The Goose with the Golden Eggs' (right).

In groups, identify the features in the story that would help you to recognize that it is a fable. Explain how the moral at the end of the tale is related to what happens in the story.

Now feed back to the class.

> **fable** a traditional tale, often involving the supernatural, whose purpose is to convey a moral lesson

The Goose with the Golden Eggs

One day a countryman going to the nest of his goose found there an egg all yellow and glittering. When he took it up it was as heavy as lead and he was going to throw it away, because he thought a trick had been played upon him. But he took it home on second thoughts, and soon found to his delight that it was an egg of pure gold. Every morning the same thing occurred, and he soon became rich by selling his eggs. As he grew rich, he grew greedy; and thinking to get at once all the gold the goose could give, he killed it and opened it only to find nothing.

Greed oft <u>o'er reaches itself</u>.[1]

[1] *defeats its object by going too far*

Introduction `as a class`

The fable that you have just studied was written hundreds of years ago. It was designed to give people at that time a warning about the way they lived, and to persuade them not to be greedy. If someone were to write a modern fable for people today, what warning do you think they would want to give people? What are we doing that is wrong and could be put right?

Forty years ago an environmentalist, Rachel Carson, wrote just such a fable at the beginning of her book *Silent Spring*. She wanted people to understand that they had to stop polluting the earth immediately or dire consequences would follow.

Carson asked her readers to imagine a world where words of warning about the effects of chemicals and pollution were not heeded. As a result, the land becomes a silent place where no birds sing, no insects buzz, where rivers are empty and nothing grows. In other words through people's greed to grow more crops, they too had killed the goose that laid the golden eggs.

As a class, read Rachel Carson's fable (**Worksheet 21**).

`as a group`

In groups, discuss these questions:

1 What features in Carson's story identify it as a fable?
2 What do you think caused the 'silent spring' that Carson describes in her fable?
3 Imagine what it would be like to live in such a world. What would you miss most?
4 Do you think it could really happen?
5 Discuss other concerns that you have about the world we live in, such as saving the rainforest, or something local, such as a park that is about to be built on. Use the first half of the planning sheet to record your ideas (**Worksheet 22**).

Development `on your own`

You are now going to write your own fable for today.

● Think about the concerns about the world that you discussed and concentrate on just one idea.
● Keep it simple, no more than 200 words.
● Use the planning frame (**Worksheet 22**) to help you structure your fable.
● Make sure that it has all the 'ingredients' of traditional fables that you have identified, including a moral at the end.

! **Remember** to read your work carefully, improve it if necessary, and write a brief comment on how well you think you have completed the task.

Plenary

What are three important features of a fable? Write them down on your whiteboard, or on a piece of paper.

`homework`

Write the final draft of your fable for homework.

Independent reading

Remember to keep up your independent reading.

Exploring the natural world

Aims

On these two pages you will:

- Explore the way in which non-fiction texts both inform and entertain their readers.
- Judge the effectiveness of a piece of non-fiction writing in terms of how it engages the interest of the reader.
- Develop your skill in using prefixes and suffixes in order to understand and spell words.

Starter  as a group

The class will be divided into six teams. Each team will be given either a prefix or a suffix. Write down as many words as you can in the time given that contain your prefix or suffix.

Prefix teams	Suffix teams
en/em	able
dis	ful
re	ive

Now discuss these questions:

1 What can you say about the meaning of your list of words that have the same prefix or suffix?

2 How can spotting prefixes and suffixes help you to spell difficult words?

Later in the lesson your teacher will test you on the spelling of some of the words that you wrote down.

Introduction as a class

So far you have been exploring the literary techniques that fiction texts use to make the writing imaginative and entertaining. But writer of non-fiction also often use these techniques. In the final part of this section you will turn your attention to the craft of these writers, focusing on books about the natural world.

Many people are interested in the natural world in a way that requires knowing something more than bare facts. Authors and natural history experts, such as David Attenborough and Gerald Durrell, provide this information in an engaging, well-written style which both informs and entertains.

Read the extract on page 31, from David Attenborough's *Life on Earth*, in which you are given information about a deadly species – the scorpion.

 in pairs

In pairs, use the questions on **Worksheet 23** to help you explore the ways in which this non-fiction text informs and entertains the reader. Feed back to the class.

Development on your own

Write a short piece in answer to this question:

How has David Attenborough tried to engage the interest of his readers in the extract on scorpions? Would you say he was successful?

Use the information that you have gathered on **Worksheet 23** to guide and structure your response.

> **!** **Remember** to read your work carefully, improve it if necessary and write a brief comment on how well you think you have completed the task.

Plenary

Write down on your whiteboard, or on a piece of paper, the three most effective methods that David Attenborough uses to entertain and inform his audience.

 Prepare to be tested on some of the difficult spellings that you met in the starter activity on prefixes and suffixes. Add them to your spelling log if necessary.

Independent reading

Remember to keep up your independent reading.

Scorpions resemble creatures, now long extinct, called sea scorpions that once terrorised the oceans. Some grew to a length of two metres and were armed with immense pincers with which they seized smaller creatures. The land scorpions were not direct descendants, but belonged to the same broad group and certainly shared the same savage habits.

The scorpions that live today have not only fearsome-looking claws but a large poison gland[1] with a sharp curving sting drooping from the end of a thin tail. Approaching such an aggressive and powerful creature is a dangerous enterprise even if the move is made by another individual of the same species. There is a real risk of it being regarded not as a mate but a meal. So scorpion mating demands the ritualised safeguards and placations of courtship.[2]

The male scorpion approaches the female with great wariness.[3] Suddenly he grabs her pincers with his. Thus linked, with her weapons neutralised,[4] the pair begin to dance. Backwards and forwards they move with their tails held upright, sometimes even intertwined. After some time, their shuffling steps have cleared the dancing ground of much of its debris.[5]

The eggs eventually hatch inside the mother's pouch, the young crawl out and clamber up on to her back. There they stay for about a fortnight until they have completed their first moult[6] and can fend for themselves.

[1] an organ in the body
[2] rituals which make mating safe
[3] care
[4] made ineffective
[5] loose material on the ground
[6] the act of shedding skin

David Attenborough was born in 1926. He is famous for enthusiastically sharing his love of the natural world through his television series such as *Life on Earth, Life in the Freezer* and *The Living Planet*. His wildlife programmes catch the imagination and attention of their audience because they are both informative and entertaining. His books accompanying the series have also encouraged people to explore the natural world further.

Making comparisons

Aims

On these two pages you will:

- Investigate the use of figurative language in an autobiography.
- Explore the way in which this author informs and entertains his readers.
- Compare two non-fiction texts on scorpions.
- Consider why authors choose a particular style in their writing.

Starter  in pairs

You have already investigated the effect of using figurative language in fiction (pages 22–23). Now you will revisit the term in the context of literary non-fiction.

In pairs, read the first paragraph of the extract on page 33. It is taken from Gerald Durrell's autobiographical book *My Family and Other Animals*, which describes how he spent his youth with his family on the Greek island of Corfu. Like Attenborough, Durrell was clearly fascinated by scorpions.

1. Write down all the examples of figurative language that you can find. (One example has been highlighted for you, to start you off.)

2. If you can, say what type of figurative language they are, for example simile, metaphor, personification.

3. What mood or tone does the author create by using figurative language in this context? (Think about the difference between this piece and the Attenborough extract on page 31.)

Be ready to feed back to the class.

Introduction in pairs

Still in pairs, read the whole of the extract on page 33. Use the questions on **Worksheet 24** to help you to explore the ways in which Durrell engages the interest of his audience.

Development in pairs

You have now studied two extracts about scorpions. However, Attenborough and Durrell have adopted their own particular style and approach to provide their readers with information. What are the similarities and differences between them?

In pairs, answer the questions on **Worksheet 25** to help you to compare the ways in which these two writers engage the interest of their readers.

Plenary

Given that Gerald Durrell and David Attenborough are both writing about scorpions, what reasons do you think there might be for the differences in style between them? (Consider first the purpose and audience of each piece of writing.)

homework

For homework, write a comparison of the techniques used by David Attenborough and Gerald Durrell to inform and entertain their readers in their descriptions of scorpions. Explain why each approach is appropriate for its intended purpose.

Use your answers to the questions on **Worksheet 25** to provide the structure and content of your comparison.

> ! **Remember** to read your work carefully, improve it if necessary, and write a brief comment on how well you think you have completed the task.

Independent reading
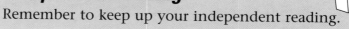

Remember to keep up your independent reading.

But the shyest and most <u>self-effacing</u>[1] of the wall community were the most dangerous; you hardly ever saw one unless you looked for it, and yet there must have been several hundred living in the cracks of the wall. Slide a knife-blade carefully under a piece of the loose plaster and lever it gently away from the brick, and there, crouching beneath it, would be a little black scorpion an inch long, looking as though he were made out of polished chocolate. They were weird-looking things, with their flattened, oval bodies, their neat, crooked legs, the enormous crab-like claws, <u>bulbous</u>[2] and neatly jointed as armour, and the tail like a string of brown beads ending in **a sting like a rose-thorn**. The scorpion would lie there quite quietly as you examined him, only raising his tail in an almost apologetic gesture of warning if you breathed too hard on him. If you kept him in the sun too long he would simply turn his back on you and walk away, and then slide slowly but firmly under another section of plaster.

I grew very fond of these scorpions. I found them to be pleasant, <u>unassuming</u>[3] creatures with, on the whole, the most charming habits. Provided you did nothing silly or clumsy (like putting your hand on one) the scorpions treated you with respect, their one desire being to get away and hide as quickly as possible. They must have found me rather a trial, for I was always ripping sections of the plaster away so that I could watch them, or capturing them and making them walk about in jam-jars so that I could see the way their feet moved. By means of my sudden and unexpected assaults on the wall I discovered quite a bit about the scorpions. I found that they would eat bluebottles (though how they caught them was a mystery I never solved), grasshoppers, moths, and lacewing flies. Several times I found them eating each other, a habit I found most distressing in a creature otherwise so <u>impeccable</u>.[4]

By crouching under the wall at night with a torch, I managed to catch some brief glimpses of the scorpions' wonderful courtship dances. I saw them standing, claws clasped, their bodies raised to the skies, their tails lovingly entwined; I saw them waltzing slowly in circles among the moss cushions, claw in claw. But my view of these performances was all too short, for almost as soon as I switched on the torch the partners would stop, pause for a moment, and then, seeing that I was not going to <u>extinguish</u>[5] the light, they would turn round and walk firmly away, claw in claw, side by side. They were definitely beasts that believed in keeping themselves to themselves. If I could have kept a colony in captivity I would probably have been able to see the whole of the courtship, but the family had forbidden scorpions in the house, despite my arguments in favour of them.

[1] modest
[2] bulb-shaped
[3] modest
[4] faultless
[5] turn off

Gerald Durrell (1925–1998) devoted himself to the study of the natural world from a young age. In his adult life, he became famous for bringing back endangered species to his zoo in Jersey in order to save them from extinction. Durrell wrote about his life and his animals in a series of interesting and humorous books.

Entertaining through humour

Aims

On these two pages you will:
- Explore different types of humour.
- Examine the ways in which non-fiction recounts can entertain through humour.
- Write a story in two different tones, one humorous, the other serious.

Starter  as a group

Each group of four will be given a word which is used to describe a type of humour (**Worksheet 26**).

1 Explore what the term means (use a dictionary to help you).

2 Think of an example that could be used to explain the meaning of this term to the rest of the class.

Introduction as a class

Gerald Durrell is famous for his humorous autobiographical accounts. His style, tone and timing help to maintain our interest and make us smile.

Read the extract from Durrell's *My Family and Other Animals* on **Worksheet 27** to find out what happened when his investigations into scorpions got out of hand.

as a group

Durrell uses several methods to create humour in his story:
- Structure and pace
- Language and tone
- Characterization
- Action and reaction.

Each group will explore one of these methods before reporting back to the class. Use the boxes below to help you.

Structure and pace

To be entertaining a story needs to be carefully structured, with just the right amount of detail at any one time, otherwise it could become boring. It also needs to move at the right pace to maintain the reader's interest.

- How does Durrell structure his story?
- Where does the pace change?
- How is the change of pace reflected in the structure of the story?

Summarize each paragraph and make a comment about what it contributes to the humour of the story. You could draw up a table like this:

Paragraph	Subject	What it contributes to the humour
Paragraph 1	Capturing the scorpion and setting up the 'matchbox' scene	A long, slow introduction which has the effect of…

Language and tone

Words need to be chosen carefully to create the right atmosphere and tone.

- How does the language of the passage contribute to its humour?
- Does the author use different types of humour? (Think back to the starter activity.)
- How would you describe the tone of the passage?

You could draw up a table like this:

Words and phrases	How these create a humorous tone
'pale fawn fur coat'	An amusing image, which also sets up the scorpion as a cuddly creature, in contrast to what follows

Characterization

Durrell's portrayal of his family, and the way in which they react to each other and the situation, plays an important role in creating humour in the story.

- Describe how each character is presented in the story.
- How do they respond to the events, and how does this contribute to the humour of the passage?
- Does the characterization of the animals add another dimension of humour?

You could draw up a table like this:

Character	How s/he contributes humour	Quotations as evidence
Larry	Very relaxed and slightly pompous at first, but then explodes with fright – a humorous contrast	'talking glibly', 'he uttered a roar of fright'
Leslie		
Margo		
Roger		
Scorpion		

Action and reaction

An essential element of an entertaining story is the content – what actually happens.

- What do you think are the funniest events in the story?
- Are these funny events examples of different types of humour? (Think back to the starter activity.)

You could draw up a table like this:

Action/event	Why it is funny	Type of humour
Margo threw a glass of water at the scorpion, which drenched her mother instead	Margo is panicking: all she does is add to the chaos of the scene	Slapstick

Development on your own

Write a short entertaining story of your own (fact or fiction) about an encounter with nature. Try to make it as humorous as you can by using the methods you have identified in the Durrell extract. You could follow this structure:

- Paragraph 1: an introduction setting the scene.
- Paragraph 2: what goes wrong.
- Paragraph 3: how this is resolved.

Plenary

Two people will be chosen to read their stories. What key features of making a story entertaining have they used?

homework

Write about the same incident for homework, and use the same structure, but this time make the tone serious rather than humorous. You will need to pay particular attention to your choice of language. What other aspects of your humorous piece will you have to change to make it serious?

! **Remember** to read your work carefully, improve it if necessary and write a brief comment on how well you think you have completed the task.

Independent reading

In the next lesson you will report back on the book you have been reading during this section. Make sure that you have finished it and bring it to the lesson.

Aims

On these two pages you will:

- Review the literary terms that you have been using in this section.
- Reflect on your independent reading and set yourself further challenges as a reader.
- Share your reading experience with other members of the class.
- Reflect on your skills in speaking and listening.

Starter *in pairs*

Review what you have learnt in this section by exploring some of the terms that you have been using.

Each pair will be given a number:

1 Focus on the pair of words with your number in the box below.

2 Explain the two terms, bringing out the difference between them.

3 If you have time, look at the other pairs of words and try to explain them.

Be prepared to feed back to the class.

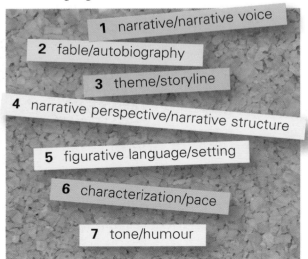

1 narrative/narrative voice

2 fable/autobiography

3 theme/storyline

4 narrative perspective/narrative structure

5 figurative language/setting

6 characterization/pace

7 tone/humour

Introduction *on your own*

At the beginning of this section you were asked to undertake some personal, independent reading of a novel, and now the time has come for you to reflect on what you have read, tell others about the book(s) you have read and find out what they have enjoyed reading too.

1 You have already recorded important facts about the book you have read and its narrative techniques on **Worksheet 12**. Now reflect further on your book by filling in **Worksheet 28**. This will also ask you to think about your next reading challenge. (You can use what you've learnt about non-fiction texts on pages 30–35 to help set new reading challenges for yourself. You may, for example, want to choose an autobiography, or a non-fiction book about the natural world.)

2 Now use both worksheets to prepare a short talk about the book that you have read, including a reading from it. The challenge is to give the other members of your group a good 'feel' for the book, which may encourage them to read it too. The contents of the worksheets will help you to organize your thoughts, but you can present your reading and talk in whichever way you think is best. Try to refer to as much of the information on **Worksheets 12** and **28** as you can.

Development `as a group`

In groups of four, each person in turn will give their reading and talk about their book. Listen carefully to each other.

After you have heard all four presentations, decide between you:

- Who gave the best reading?
- Who gave the most interesting talk?
- Which book would the group most like to read?

Be prepared to report back to the class.

! **Remember** that when you are speaking and listening you need to:

- Have something of interest to say and know when the time is right to talk.
- Be able to speak with expression, in a variety of tones, appropriate to the context.
- Show that you can listen patiently and carefully to what others have to say, even if you don't agree with them.
- Be able to respond to and develop points made by others.
- Encourage other people to speak and develop their ideas.

Now reflect on your skills in speaking and listening by completing **Worksheet 29**. Remember to set yourself some challenging targets.

Plenary

Your teacher will ask members of the class what their next book choice is.

- What features of their independent reading book have led to this choice?
- Has anyone chosen a literary non-fiction work, and if so why?

homework

Using **Worksheets 12** and **28** write a short piece of between 200 and 400 words explaining how the author of your independent reading book has maintained your interest as a reader.

! **Remember** to read your work carefully, improve it if necessary, and write a brief comment on how well you think you have completed the task.

Reviewing what's been learnt

In this section you have:

- Developed your skills as a reader by exploring the way in which authors of fiction and non-fiction engage the interest of their readers.
- Learnt about and used technical literary terms such as narrative perspective and figurative language.
- Studied how and why authors introduce themes into their books.
- Examined the structure of a novel.
- Used writer's techniques in your own imaginative writing.
- Read a substantial text independently and shared your opinions on it with others.
- Set yourself reading challenges for the future.
- Reflected on your skills as a contributor to group discussion and in making a formal presentation.

Now it's time to think about what things you have learnt from this section, and list the key points in your exercise book, using the following sentence starters to help you:

The key things I have learnt about writing in this section are ...

I now understand more about ...

When presenting ideas, I now know ...

Some of the vocabulary I now feel more confident about using is ...

The words I have learnt to spell are ...

The things I found most difficult were ...

The things I think I did best were ...

I now feel more confident about ...

My targets to improve my work are: (include reading, writing, spelling, speaking and listening)

-
-
-
-
-
-

Inform, explain, describe

Introduction

You should already be familiar with the right language for informing, explaining and describing. This year you will learn to recognize and use this language more expertly, both as readers and writers. The topics you will focus on are 'Starting Shakespeare' and 'Information and reference texts'.

William Shakespeare is the most famous playwright in the world. Even though he died nearly four hundred years ago, countless people watch his plays being performed in theatres all around the world, and many students at schools and colleges study his writing. Next year you will study one of his plays for your end of Key Stage 3 tests.

People are not only interested in Shakespeare's plays; they also want to find out about where he lived, about his family and what life was like when he was alive, so that they can get more out of his writing. Information and reference texts, including electronic forms of information such as the internet, are the most common sources of this kind of information.

Key aims

- To develop fluency as readers and writers of information and reference texts.
- To present information effectively, to explain complex ideas and to use formal language to describe.

Introducing Shakespeare

Aims

On these two pages you will:

- Develop your skills as active, critical readers of various modern and contemporary texts about Shakespeare and his times.
- Practise using the apostrophe of possession correctly.

Starter · on your own

As you know, apostrophes are used for two purposes: to show where a letter or letters have been missed out of a word (the apostrophe of omission) and to show possession or ownership (the apostrophe of possession).

There are three main rules about how to use the apostrophe of possession:

- **When the word is singular**, you add an apostrophe + *s* for the possessive form: *the man's face, James's turn.*
- **When the word is plural and already ends in *s***, you add an apostrophe to the end of the word for the possessive form: *your parents' house, a boys' school.*
- **When the word is plural but it doesn't end in *s***, you add an apostrophe + *s* for the possessive form: *women's clothes, children's books.*

Your teacher is going to read you some sentences (**Worksheet 30**). Get out your whiteboards and listen to the instructions.

objective based on fact and reason, unbiased, not influenced by personal feelings

subjective influenced by personal feelings and opinion, biased

Introduction

William Shakespeare was born in Stratford upon Avon in 1564 and died in 1616. He spent most of his adult life in London, where he worked his way up from actor to writer to owner of the theatre where his plays were performed. Having made his money, he retired to Stratford. He is believed to have written 39 plays as well as many fine poems.

Your teacher will read you two sources of information on Shakespeare's life (**Worksheet 31**). Ben Jonson was a friend of Shakespeare, so his judgement of Shakespeare's importance and reputation is personal or **subjective**. The encyclopedia is a more impersonal or **objective** source of information.

in pairs

In pairs, discuss the following questions:

1 Jonson calls Shakespeare 'the wonder of our stage'. What does he mean by this?

2 Why does he think Shakespeare shouldn't be put alongside (or classed with) Spenser, Chaucer and Beaumont?

3 He describes Shakespeare as a 'Moniment without a tombe'. What do you think this metaphor means?

4 He describes Shakespeare as being 'alive still'? In what sense do you think Shakespeare could be alive?

5 What facts do you learn about Shakespeare's life from the encyclopedia extract?

6 What opinions are expressed in the extract?

7 Why are the opinions so outnumbered by the facts?

Be prepared to feed back to the class.

Development *in pairs*

Worksheet 32 contains a contemporary account by Thomas Dekker of life in Shakespeare's London, and two extracts from Susan Cooper's novel *King of Shadows*, which tells the story of a young boy, Nat, who is transported back to Shakespeare's time.

In pairs, read all the extracts and then answer the following questions:

1 The authors of the extracts use lots of sensual imagery of smells and sounds to describe Shakespeare's London. Draw up a table of smells and sounds like the one below, and describe what effect they create. (Try to include two smells and four sounds.)

Smells and sounds	Effect created
1. 'carts and coaches make such a thundering'	The noise of the traffic is like thunder: the alliteration of 'carts and coaches' and the assonance of 'such a thundering' help to make a sound picture of what Dekker is describing.

2 Dekker also uses powerful verbs and similes to describe the movement of people in the streets of London. Find two examples of each from the text and explain how they help to paint a picture of the scene.

3 Cooper uses **alliteration** in her writing, for example 'carts clattered over the cobbles, creaking'. What does this technique add to her picture of London?

4 In both extracts she also uses lists, for example 'creaking, rocking, splashing up muck'. What effect do these lists have?

5 What have you learnt about Shakespeare's London from the three extracts?

6 Cooper's novel was published in 1999. Is this **source** more or less reliable as an account of London during Shakespeare's time than Dekker's description, which was written by someone who was alive at the time?

alliteration the effect created when words next to or close to each other begin with the same letter or sound: 'several silent slithering snakes'
source a text or document that provides evidence; also, a text used by an author to help them in their own writing

Plenary

On your whiteboard or a piece of paper, jot down three key things that you have learned so far about William Shakespeare, and three key things about what London was like during his lifetime.

Starting Macbeth

Aims

On these two pages you will:

- Explore how witches are presented in Shakespeare's *Macbeth*, and compare this with contemporary views on witches.
- Recognize how a historical text differs in sentence structure, vocabulary and tone from a modern text.

Starter  in pairs

Your teacher will read you an extract from King James I's book on witches, entitled *Daemonologie*, which was written in Shakespeare's time (**Worksheet 33**). What do you notice about its vocabulary, sentence structure and tone?

In pairs, draw up a table like the one below. List six words in the first column and give their modern spelling and/or meaning in the second column. Then give two examples of unusual sentence structure, and describe in the second column how a modern text would structure the sentence differently.

Example	Modern spelling/meaning
1. aboundinge	abounding (= rapid increase in numbers)

Discuss how you would describe the tone of this text. In what way would the tone of a modern book on witches be different?

Be prepared to feed back to the class.

Introduction

Shakespeare's play *Macbeth*, which was probably written in 1606 when James I was king, tells the story of an ambitious Scottish soldier called Macbeth. A group of witches or 'weird sisters' predict that he will be made Thane of Cawdor (a nobleman), and this indeed happens. He then uses violence to make their second prophecy, that he will become king, come true. After gaining the crown, however, things start to go downhill for him.

in pairs

In this lesson you are going to explore how the witches are presented in *Macbeth*, and what both Shakespeare and his contemporaries thought about witches.

Worksheet 33 contains two sources that provide information about people's attitudes to witches in Shakespeare's time. Read these in pairs, and discuss the questions underneath the extracts.

Development **as a class**

Now read the extract from *Macbeth* on page 43 and discuss the following questions:

1. What had the sailor's wife done to annoy the witches?
2. How do the witches plan to punish the sailor?
3. What does Shakespeare tell us about the appearance of the witches? Quote phrases from the text to support your answer.
4. Are the witches presented as threatening, fearful creatures, or as malicious old ladies? Give

evidence for your view.

5 Why, according to Banquo, do these 'instruments of darkness' sometimes tell us good news?

6 From all this information, do you think Shakespeare shares the views of his contemporaries about witchcraft? Explain your answer.

Plenary

Jot down on your whiteboards, or on a piece of paper, three things that you have learnt about witches in Shakespeare's time.

In this extract from Act I scene 3 of *Macbeth*, set on a 'blasted heath', the witches are planning to attack a sailor whose wife has annoyed them. Macbeth and his companion, Banquo, come across the witches, and Banquo gives his reaction to them.

Thunder. Enter the three **Witches**

FIRST WITCH Where hast thou been, sister?
SECOND WITCH Killing swine.
THIRD WITCH Sister, where thou?
FIRST WITCH A sailor's wife had chestnuts
    in her lap,
  And munch'd, and munch'd, and munch'd.
  'Give me,' quoth[1] I.
  'Aroint thee,[2] witch!' the rump-fed ronyon[3]
  cries.
  Her husband's to Aleppo gone, master o'
    th' Tiger:[4]
  But in a sieve I'll thither sail,
  And, like a rat without a tail,
  I'll do, I'll do, and I'll do.
SECOND WITCH I'll give thee a wind.
FIRST WITCH Th'art kind.
THIRD WITCH And I another.
FIRST WITCH I myself have all the other;
  And the very ports they blow,
  All th' quarters[5] that they know
  I' th' shipman's card.
  I will drain him dry as hay:[6]
  Sleep shall neither night nor day
  Hang upon his pent-house lid;[7]
  He shall live a man forbid:[8]
  Weary sev'nights,[9] nine times nine

  Shall he dwindle, peak,[10] and pine.
25   Though his bark[11] cannot be lost,
  Yet it shall be tempest-tost.
  Look what I have.
SECOND WITCH Show me, show me.
FIRST WITCH Here I have a pilot's thumb,
30   Wreck'd as homeward he did come.
Drum within
  THIRD WITCH A drum, a drum!
  Macbeth doth come.
ALL The Weird Sisters, hand in hand,
  Posters[12] of the sea and land,
35   Thus do go about, about;
  Thrice to thine, and thrice to mine,
  And thrice again, to make up nine.
  Peace! the charm's wound up.
Enter **Macbeth** *and* **Banquo**
  BANQUO   ... What are these
40   So wither'd, and so wild in their attire,
  That look not like th' inhabitants o' th' earth,
  And yet are on't? Live you, or are you ought
  That man may question?[13] You seem to
    understand me,
  By each at once her choppy[14] finger laying
45   Upon her skinny lips. You should be women,
  And yet your beards forbid me to interpret
  That you are so ...
        But 'tis strange;
  And oftentimes to win us to our harm,
50   The instruments of darkness tell us truths,
  Win us with honest trifles, to betray's
  In deepest consequence.[15]

---

[6] because he won't be able to land to get water supplies
[7] eyelid
[8] cursed
[9] weeks
[10] become thin
[11] ship
[12] creatures that can travel quickly
[13] beings that man can talk to
[14] chapped
[15] to deceive us with important consequences

ut
w
ame of the ship
s of the compass

Investigating witches

Aims

On these two pages you will:

- Develop your research skills, using ICT and books, to find out about witches in Shakespeare's time.
- Investigate how new words are formed, and use this knowledge to help you with their spelling and meaning.

Starter *as a class*

New words are being formed all the time, especially those relating to new technology. Looking at how new words are formed can help you to understand their meaning and to spell them correctly.

- Many new words are formed by adding prefixes or suffixes, for example:
  internet = inter + net;
  hypertext = hyper + text.
- Others are **portmanteau words**, which run together two existing words to form a new one, for example:
  home page = home + page;
  newsgroup = news + group.
- Often portmanteau words run together the first part of the first word with the last part of the second word, for example:
  netiquette = net(work) + (et)iquette.
- Finally, many new words are **clipped forms** of older words, for example:
  web is short for *World Wide Web.*

In pairs, fill in the grid on **Worksheet 34**, which lists several new words relating to new technology.

 Add to your spelling log any words that you find difficult to spell. Make a note of how they are formed, to help you remember how to spell them.

clipped form a word formed from the reduction of another word: 'phone' from 'telephone'
portmanteau word a word formed by running together or blending two words: 'smog' from 'smoke' + 'fog'

Introduction *as a class*

This lesson you are going to work in groups to research witchcraft in Shakespeare's time. In two lessons' time you are going to use this research to write a leaflet on witchcraft.

Fill in the first column of the KWL grid on **Worksheet 35** on your own. Then fill in the second column as a class. You will fill in the third column at the end of your research (page 49).

What do I already know?	What do I want to know?	What have I learnt?
James I wrote a book about witches called 'Daemonologie'	How were witches punished?	

Development *as a group*

Your teacher will assign a topic area from the second column of the KWL grid to each group, and recommend websites and books to help you with your research. Can you think of any other sources of information that you can use?

In your groups, everyone should be given specific tasks to complete. Try to make use of the different abilities and talents of your group members. You may like to divide the research along these lines:

- **Internet research.** See Top Tip box (right).
- **Text-based research.** Remember to skim and scan texts to locate the relevant information that you need.
- **Drawing illustrations and diagrams.** Roughly sketch any important or interesting visual material. You can do fair copies later if you decide to use the illustration in your leaflet.

Use the notetaking frame on **Worksheet 36** to help you record the information that you find. The copy of this worksheet below shows you the function of each section.

> **! Top Tip: Researching on the internet**
>
> - Use a **search engine** to search for information. You will have to type key words into a box and then the engine will search the web for relevant information. If you include a + sign between the words, for example 'Shakespeare+witchcraft', it will only search for websites with a connection between the words. This will result in a long list of possible sites you can investigate. The first sites listed are usually the most relevant ones.
> - Use **hypertext links** to leap between different pages and websites as you search for more information. Make sure you write down the name of the website (it's usually on the home page), so that you can find it again. Bookmark good pages as 'favourites' on the toolbar. And remember to acknowledge website information as a source, by giving the name of the site in your bibliography.

Plenary

When you have collected the information, feed back to each other what you have found out about your research topics. Discuss what further research needs to be done for homework.

homework

Continue researching your topic for homework.

The topic you are researching, for example 'Witch hunts'.

Research question:	
Source 1:	
Key points:	

Make a note of the source of your information here (title and author of the text). You must acknowledge the sources in a bibliography at the end of your leaflet.

Make your notes here. Only make notes relevant to the topic you are researching, and keep them brief and clear.

Explaining your research

Aims

On these two pages you will:

- Review the features of explanation texts.
- Write an explanation of how computers can help you with research.
- Explore different methods of grouping sentences into paragraphs.

Starter
as a class

One feature of well-written texts is that they have good paragraphing. Sentences can be grouped into paragraphs in various different ways, for example:

- By expanding on the point made in the opening sentence of the paragraph
- By adding examples ('For example …')
- By modifying the point made in the opening sentence of the paragraph ('However …')
- By chronology ('First … then …').

In each case, the opening sentence will signal the purpose of the paragraph, and all the sentences in that paragraph will work towards that purpose.

Listen while your teacher reads you an extract from a book for students on Media Studies, in which the authors discuss various issues relating to the practical production that students have to submit as part of their GCSE coursework (**Worksheet 37**). Then, as a class, fill in the grid on **Worksheet 38** to analyse how the sentences have been organized into paragraphs.

Introduction
in pairs

Your task in this lesson is to write an explanation of how computers can help you with research. First, therefore, review in pairs the key features of explanation texts, focusing on the following:

- Purpose – what are they for?
- Structure – how are the paragraphs ordered?
- Style – e.g. what voice and tense are used?
- Presentation – how important are diagrams and layout?

Be prepared to feed back to the class.

Development
as a group

Now it is time to put your knowledge of explanation texts into effect. You are going to write an explanation, to your grandparents, of how computers can help you with research.

In groups, brainstorm ideas using **Worksheet 39**. Think about how you used the internet and other new technology when you researched witches in Shakespeare's time, but you shouldn't restrict yourself to this. The question is a general one, so you can use your experience at other times to provide different examples.

You may be using several words or ideas that your audience will not understand. Use the worksheet to note these words down.

on your own

Now write your explanation, in no more than eight paragraphs. Follow the steps in the flow chart on page 47 to help you.

Your first paragraph should introduce the subject to the reader in an interesting way, e.g.:

So you think computers are useless? I'm going to explain how useful they really are ...

Organize the ideas that you have brainstormed into paragraphs, with each paragraph clearly indicating what point it is making in the first sentence, as you saw in the starter activity, e.g.:

Another reason why computers are so useful when you research is ...

Remember to give examples to back up your explanation, e.g.:

For example, when I wanted to research witches ...

End by relating the subject to the reader, or referring back to the introduction, e.g.:

So can you see now how useful computers have been ...

You should explain any difficult words as you go, or put the explanation in a glossary at the end, e.g.:

website: a collection of pages or documents on the internet that relate to a particular topic

Plenary

Swap your first draft with a partner's. Does it contain the key features of an explanation text, as discussed in the introduction activity?

! **Remember** to read your work carefully, pretending to know nothing about the subject. Is it clear? Improve it if necessary and write a brief comment on how well you think you have completed the task.

homework

Complete your explanation for homework.

Writing your leaflet

Aims

On these two pages you will:

- Write up your research on witches as an information leaflet suitable for Year 8 students.
- Practise using participles as a way of combining clauses into complex sentences.

Starter

Your research notes will probably be in abbreviated form, and the sentences will lack linking words. Later in the lesson you will need to use your notes to write clear but interesting continuous text. How do you get from notes to finished text?

You have already learnt how to make your writing more interesting by using connectives and subordinate clauses. One way of combining clauses is to use **participles**.

Imagine that you had taken this note as part of your research:

> Witch hunts common – makes it impossible for accused to get justice.

When you write up your notes you could use a participle to combine the two bits of information:

> Witch hunts were common, _making_ it impossible for the accused to get justice.

Note the comma, which acts as a signpost to tell you that there is a new clause – here introduced by the participle.

The sentences on **Worksheet 40** have been cut up into their clauses. In pairs, match a main clause to a clause beginning with a participle, so that you end up with seven sentences that make sense.

- Can you identify the participle in each sentence?
- Does it make any difference if the main clause begins or ends the sentence?
- What punctuation would you add to each sentence to make it clearer?

Be prepared to feed back to the class.

participle a form of the verb that can help to form a clause. _Present participles_ are formed by adding '-ing' to the base form of regular verbs: 'needing', 'helping'. _Past participles_ are formed by adding '-ed' to the base form of regular verbs: 'needed', 'helped'; many are irregular and have other endings: 'flown', 'kept', 'written'.

Introduction

You are now going to prepare a written assignment based on your research. Each group should produce an information leaflet on witches, suitable for Year 8 students.

In your groups, write up and present the material that you have researched, using the title of your topic as the heading for your leaflet.

Before you plan your leaflet, discuss as a class what are the important features of information texts. Think about the following issues:

- **Purpose**
- **Structure** (overall structure, paragraphing, use of connectives ...)
- **Style** (sentence structure, formality of language, vocabulary, tense, person ...)
- **Presentation** (layout, headings, illustrations ...).

as a group

Begin by planning the overall structure of your leaflet so that it fits together in a coherent way. What information will you include? Record your thoughts on the planning grid (**Worksheet 41**). Each member of the group should be responsible for part of the leaflet.

Now discuss how you can present the information so that it is appropriate for Year 8 readers. Visual material is obviously going to be a feature of the leaflet. Jot down your thoughts in the relevant section of the planning grid.

Development *on your own*

Thinking about all the factors discussed so far in this lesson, draft your leaflet, remembering to use appropriate language and layout so that it appeals to other Year 8 students.

Show your draft to another group and ask them to comment on it. Then check and complete your draft.

You may find it helpful to write your draft on computer, using a desk-top publishing programme, as it will save you time and will be easy to edit.

Plenary

What have you learnt about your topic and how to research it? Fill in the final column on the KWL grid (**Worksheet 34**).

homework

Write the final version of your part of the leaflet for homework.

> ! **Remember** to read through your work carefully, thinking about the audience and purpose of your writing. Improve it if necessary and write a brief comment saying how well you think you have completed the task.

Presenting your leaflet

Aims

On these two pages you will:

- Work together as a group to present your leaflet to another group.
- Evaluate your skills in speaking, listening and in group discussion.
- Explore how some texts are more formal than others.

Starter

When you write or speak, the language and grammatical structures that you use vary in several ways depending on what you are writing or saying, and the people you are writing or speaking to. One way in which they vary is how formal or informal they are.

- **Formal language** is used in job interviews, to give the news on TV, and for serious writing. It almost always uses Standard English, and avoids slang and colloquialisms.
- **Informal language** uses more relaxed language and grammatical structures, such as **contractions** and sentences without a subject or a verb. Tabloid newspapers and some teachers introducing a lesson use informal language.
- **Colloquial language** is the language used in conversation. It has a much looser structure and may include slang and dialect words.

in pairs

In pairs, read the extracts on **Worksheet 42**, and put them in order of formality. What clues did you use to decide how formal or informal each extract was? Where do you think each extract came from: a book, a newspaper, the internet, a magazine?

Be prepared to feed back your ideas.

Introduction as a group

This lesson you are going to deliver a short presentation about your leaflet to another group, explaining how you went about the research, how you organized your group so that everybody contributed to the final product, what you learnt about witches in Shakespeare's time and what you learnt about producing a leaflet. The presentation should not last more than five minutes, but each person in the group must speak.

Get back into your leaflet-writing groups and prepare your presentation by discussing the following questions:

- How will you structure your presentation? Will each of you present your own part of the leaflet, covering all the issues outlined above? Or will one of you speak about how you researched, another about how you organized the group and so on?
- How will you use any visual aids? Can you think of any, apart from the leaflet itself?
- What kind of language will you use in your presentation? Think back to the starter activity.

contraction the shortening of a word or words: 'she'll' is a contraction of 'she will'

- Will you present without notes, or use key words jotted onto cards to help you?
- How will you introduce and conclude the presentation?

Now rehearse your presentation and discuss how you could make improvements.

Development *as a group*

Each group will give their presentation to another group, and spend one minute answering any questions that the audience may have. The second group then gives its own presentation.

on your own

Use the self-assessment sheet on **Worksheet 43** to evaluate the strengths and weaknesses of your speaking and listening skills. Note that the presentations as such will not be evaluated: instead, you will think about your own contribution as a speaker in the presentation, and in all the group discussions that have led to this presentation (including those when you discussed writing the leaflet).

When you are considering your skills as a speaker, think whether:
- You spoke clearly and fluently
- You made eye contact with the audience or read from your notes
- You used formal language with confidence
- You used interesting vocabulary and spoke with expression.

Set yourself a target for improvement to try to achieve next time you speak as part of a presentation.

When you are considering your skills as a listener, think whether:
- You can listen carefully so that you hear and understand everything that is said
- You respect the needs of the speaker when you listen
- You show that you have listened carefully by the comments and questions that you make afterwards.

Set yourself a target for improvement to try to achieve next time you listen to a talk or presentation.

When you are considering your skills in group discussion, think whether:
- You put your own views clearly and confidently in group discussion
- You listen to other people's ideas even if you don't agree with them
- You show your understanding of other people's ideas, and sensitivity to them, in your comments and questions
- You help others to talk by asking them questions and developing their ideas.

Set yourself a target for improvement to try to achieve next time you take part in a group discussion.

Plenary

Which three targets have you focused on in order to improve your speaking and listening activities?

Be prepared to share these with a partner.

Visiting Shakespeare's London

Aims

On these two pages you will:

- Analyse different non-fiction texts relating to London landmarks.
- Write your own descriptions, adapting the formality of style to the particular audience and purpose of the text.
- Consider what listening skills are required when you listen to directions.

Starter *on your own*

On **Worksheet 44** you will find a map of part of central London. Your teacher will read out a set of directions, telling you how to get from one part of the map to another. Listen carefully to what your teacher has to say and highlight the route on your map.

as a class

You are constantly using your skills as listeners in many different situations, including listening to instructions. What strategies did you use when you were doing this activity to help you get it right?

Introduction *as a class*

Your teacher will read you the texts on page 53, which are about tourist attractions in London.

Discuss the following questions as a class:

1 What is the purpose and audience of each of these texts?
2 What types of text are they (for example, explanation, persuasion, information ...)?
3 What features of each text tell you what type it is? Think about their structure, style, person and **register**.
4 What register of language are the texts written in? What words indicate this to you?
5 What kind of visitor do you think would visit each attraction? Explain your answer with reference to information in the text.

register the level of formality of language used, such as colloquial, formal, official etc

Development *in pairs*

In pairs, decide on a building or area near you that you both know well. One of you is going to describe it in one paragraph of formal text as if you were compiling a travel guide for visitors to the area. Meanwhile your partner, pretending to be one of those visitors, will write a postcard home describing their visit to the building.

Before you begin, discuss together how your two descriptions will differ in terms of the formality of their language. Bearing in mind the purpose and audience of each text, consider how the following features of your text will differ from that of your partner's:

- Type of connectives used, if any
- Appropriate vocabulary and register
- Sentence structure
- Use of active or passive
- First, second or third person.

Now write your description, including as many of these features as is appropriate.

> **Remember** to read your work carefully, thinking about the audience and purpose of your writing. Improve it if necessary, and write a brief comment on how well you think you have completed the task.

Plenary

Your teacher will ask for two volunteers to read out their descriptions. What features of the writing tell you whether they are formal or informal descriptions?

1

Shakespeare's Globe Exhibition

Shakespeare's Globe Exhibition is the most exciting place to explore Shakespeare's theatre and the London where he lived and worked. It is the world's only permanent exhibition dedicated to the conditions under which Shakespeare's plays were first written, performed and published.

Explore Bankside, the Soho of Elizabethan London, follow Sam Wanamaker's struggle to recreate an <u>authentic</u>[1] Globe for the 20th century and beyond, and take a fascinating guided tour of today's working theatre.

An exhibition visit and tour lasts about one-and-a-half hours.

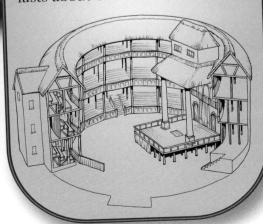

[1] *realistic, genuine*

2

Southwark Cathedral
The church did not become a cathedral until 1905. However, some parts date back to the 12th century, when the building was attached to a priory, and many of its medieval features remain. The memorials are fascinating. The wooden <u>effigy</u>[1] of a knight is late 13th century, and another gem is the tomb, dating from 1408, of John Gower, poet and contemporary of Geoffrey Chaucer.

London Dungeon
In effect a much expanded version of the chamber of horrors at Madame Tussaud's, this museum is a great hit with ghoulish children. It illustrates the most bloodthirsty events in British history. It is played strictly for terror, and screams and moans abound as Druids perform a human sacrifice at Stonehenge, Anne Boleyn is beheaded on the orders of her husband Henry VIII, and a room full of people die in agony during the Great Plague of 1665. Torture, murder and witchcraft fill the gaps between these spectacles.

[1] *sculpture*

3

London, one of the true great cities in the world. Steeped in history and tradition not to mention a thriving nightlife, spectacular West End shows, world-renowned shopping as well as numerous historic monuments, memorials and buildings. Our City sightseeing buses operate on 5 different routes taking in all that makes London great. The main start point for our red bus is situated between Piccadilly Circus and Leicester Square in the bustling Coventry Street.

The essential tour of the sights and sounds of the history and <u>pageantry</u>[1] of London – Trafalgar Square, Buckingham Palace, Westminster Abbey, the Houses of Parliament, Big Ben, Downing Street, Whitehall, St. Paul's Cathedral, Tower Bridge, the Tower of London ... and much more. It's all here, so don't forget your cameras!

[1] *ceremonies*

Aims

On these two pages you will:

- Investigate the features of CD-ROM texts, and consider their effectiveness as research tools.
- Compare Shakespeare's theatre with that of today, and write an explanation of how they differ.
- Practise using subordinate clauses.

Starter *in pairs*

You are going to start this lesson by practising how to use subordinate clauses.

Each pair will be given eight cards with clauses on them, and five cards with subordinating conjunctions (**Worksheet 45**). Your challenge is to make as many sentences as possible by combining two of the clauses with a subordinating conjunction, for example:

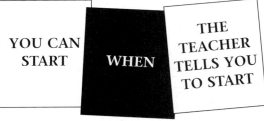

YOU CAN START — WHEN — THE TEACHER TELLS YOU TO START

You may want to use cards more than once, so write down your sentences as you make them.

- Which part of the sentence is the subordinate clause? How do you know?
- Does it make any difference if the main clause begins or ends the sentence?
- What punctuation would you add to each sentence to make it clearer?

Be prepared to feed back to the class.

Introduction *as a class*

Reference texts also come in the form of CD-ROMs. A CD-ROM is a disk which can be read by a computer. It can contain not only written information but also moving and still images and sound. Look at the two extracts on page 55. They are from a CD-ROM about *Macbeth*.

Discuss these questions as a class:

1 What features are available on these screens? How do these differ from features in a book?

2 How do you 'read' the text of a CD-ROM? How does this differ from reading the text of a book?

3 CD-ROMs are interactive texts. Does this make them more effective than books as sources of information?

in pairs

The CD-ROM extracts on page 55 describe the costume, sets and scenery of Shakespeare's theatre. In pairs, think about how these features differ from today's theatre. Summarize these differences in the grid on **Worksheet 46**.

Development *on your own*

Using the information that you have collected on **Worksheet 46**, write a short explanation of how the theatre today differs from the theatre in Shakespeare's time. You may need to remind yourself of the features of an explanation text (see page 46).

Plenary

If you had the choice of researching a topic by looking on a CD-ROM or in a book, which would you choose? Explain your answer.

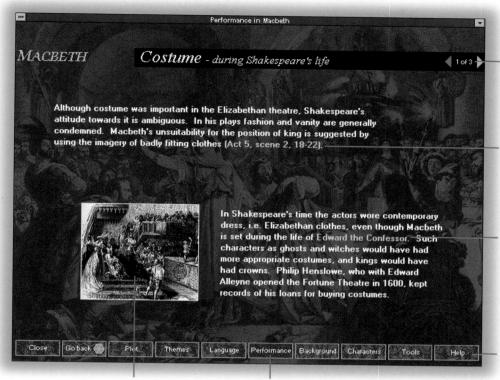

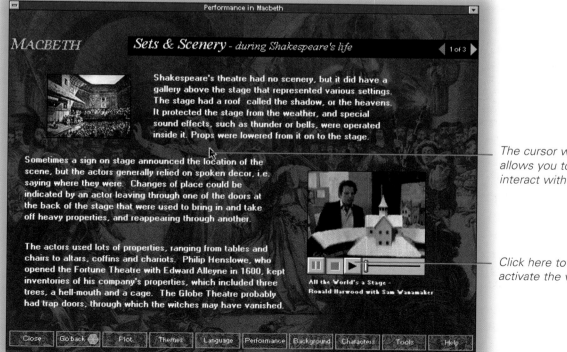

Click here to move forward or backward through the 'Costume' section

Click here to hear an audio playing of these lines

Click here to find out about Edward the Confessor

Click any of the menu options to be taken to the relevant section of the CD-ROM

Click on the photo to enlarge it

The section you are currently in is highlighted

The cursor which allows you to interact with the text

Click here to activate the video

Researching a tourist brochure

Aims

On these two pages you will:
- Analyse the kind of writing that a tourist brochure contains.
- Use your research and writing skills to plan a tourist brochure of your own, together with an explanation of how you did it.

Starter *in pairs*

Your teacher will read the two extracts from a tourist brochure on page 57. What kind of texts are these? In pairs, fill in the analysis grid on **Worksheet 47**.

Be prepared to feed back to the class.

Introduction *as a group*

In the final two lessons of this section you are going to use all the research and writing skills that you have practised so far to research, plan and write a short tourist brochure of your own, *either* for your home town *or* for Shakespeare's home town of Stratford upon Avon.

In groups of three, your task in the brochure is to:
- **Inform** visitors about three or four places to visit and/or things to do. (Include addresses, phone numbers and other important information, as in Extract A.)
- **Describe** one or two of these places or activities in a more extensive and interesting way. (Use the kind of structure and descriptive writing you identified in Extract B.)

- **Explain**, in a detailed statement, how the group researched and produced the brochure. (What was the purpose of the task? How did you allocate the work? What difficulties did you encounter in the research, writing and production? Take the reader through the process, step by step.)

First of all, in your groups of three, discuss what you are going to cover in your brochure, who is to do what task and where you are going to research the information. Use the planning frame on **Worksheet 48** to help you plan your brochure.

Development *as a group*

Research your brochure. Your teacher will help you by providing information about relevant websites. The person responsible for writing the detailed explanation should make notes on how the members of the group do their research. If they have time, they can help the other members of their group with their research.

Plenary

What difficulties have groups encountered in their planning or research? Make use of a class discussion to help solve these problems.

homework

Write a first draft of your part of the brochure, or of your explanatory statement, for homework. Before you begin writing, think about the features of texts that inform, explain or describe.

Historic Houses

FRAMPTON COURT

Frampton on Severn

Tel: 01452 740267 (home)

Grade I listed building. 2 miles off M5 junction 13. The house has been lived in by the same family since 1732. A perfect example of a Georgian stately home, with original porcelain, furniture and tapestries, and containing the paintings from the 'Frampton Flora', a bestselling book in 1985. English Heritage Grade I listed garden of special historic interest. Ornamental canal reflects the Orangery, a superb 'Strawberry Hill Gothic' building. Dutch influence. The Orangery now converted to holiday accommodation. Also tall octagonal 17th century dovecote. Gardens suitable for disabled.

Open: All year by appointment

Admission: £4.50 (children half price). Guided tour by owner. Catering facilities available to groups by prior arrangement.

Map ref: D3 OS 162/750078

B

The ghosts of Owlpen

Owlpen, a 900-year-old gabled manor house, stands peacefully at the head of a picturesque wooded valley in the Cotswolds, near Uley. But all is not what it seems, for Owlpen is one of the most haunted houses in Gloucestershire. It is traditionally home to at least four ghosts.

The most famous is that of Queen Margaret of Anjou, queen of Henry VI, who visited on her way to the battle of Tewkesbury on 2nd May 1471. It is said that her last happy night was spent at Owlpen, and she seems reluctant to leave to this day. The manor is open to visitors in the summer. If you tread softly, you may join those who have glimpsed the phantom of the <u>ardent</u>[1] queen, a grey lady clad in fur-trimmed gown, steeple hat and <u>wimple</u>,[2] haunting the 'Queen's Chamber'.

Owlpen is also home to a hooded figure, the 'Black Monk', whose quarters are in the older east wing. Sometimes he is said to be a member of the de Olepenne family, who lived in the manor in the 1100s; one of them is known to have died as a monk of St Peter's Abbey in Gloucester. Others say he was a monk fleeing from the sack of Kingswood Abbey, who was walled up and starved to death in the manor; the monk's bones apparently crumbled to dust when the space came to light, as the measurement of the rooms was found not to <u>tally</u>.[3]

Other ghosts include a mischievous child, who repeatedly runs up and down the back stairs, disturbing the tranquil sleep of guests. Many of the guests continue to relate the presence of unexplained sights and sounds – and even scents. But the occupants, Nicholas and Karin Mander and their five children, claim their sleep is ever undisturbed.

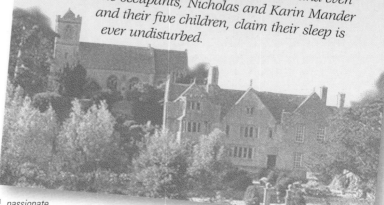

[1] *passionate*
[2] *headdress*
[3] *match, fit*

Putting your brochure together

Aims

On these two pages you will:

- Take different roles in discussing the work you have completed so far on your brochure.
- Write the final draft of the brochure and put it together.
- Adapt a descriptive information text so that it becomes a straightforward information text.

Starter *in pairs*

Read the extract from the tourist brochure on 'The world of Shakespeare' on page 59. What kind of text is this? How do you know?

Your teacher will model for you how to adapt this text so that it gives more straightforward information. The first sentence, for example, could look like this:

Stratford-upon-Avon. A historic town associated with Shakespeare.

In pairs, rewrite this text on **Worksheet 49** so that it gives straightforward information for the visitor, in no more than the space provided on the worksheet.

Report back to the class on how you adapted the text. What features of information texts have you included in your rewrite?

Introduction *as a group*

This lesson you are going to put the final touches to your brochure. First, though, you are going to discuss each other's drafts in pairs before reporting back to the group on what you found.

- The person writing the *information* should read the *description* draft and discuss it with the writer.
- The person writing the *description* should read the *explanation* draft and discuss it with the writer.
- The person writing the *explanation* should read the *information* draft and discuss it with the writer.

In each case, ask yourself if the writing works as information, description or explanation. Feed back constructive comments to the writer.

Now report back your findings to the group of three. Reach agreement on what needs to be changed.

Development *on your own*

Write or word process the final draft of your part of the brochure, taking into account the results of the discussion that you had.

as a group

Now put the brochure together. Plan the layout carefully and take care with the presentation.

Plenary

Present your brochure to the class, explaining the information you have included and why you think it is an effective brochure.

The world of Shakespeare

Beautifully situated on the river, Stratford-upon-Avon has strong links with Shakespeare and a blend of heritage and drama. This is where the bard[1] was born, lived and lies buried and there are five fascinating Shakespeare Houses which are open to visitors all year round. Three are in town, and two are just a few miles away. All of them can be explored via hop-on, hop-off Guide Friday buses.

In town, enter the Tudor world in Shakespeare's Birthplace – recently transformed to offer a fresh perspective on his early life. Hall's Croft, the home of his daughter, is one of the finest half-timbered gabled[2] houses in the town. Nash's house, the home of his granddaughter, contains an exceptional collection of 17th century oak furniture and tapestries. The house lies next to the foundations of New Place, where he spent his final years.

The other Shakespeare Houses lie in two picturesque villages just out of town. Mary Arden's House, the rambling Tudor farmhouse which belonged to Shakespeare's mother, lies in Wilmcote. Anne Hathaway's cottage, the thatched cottage and garden belonging to Shakespeare's wife, nestles[3] in Shottery.

Back in town, a gentle stroll along the River Avon leads to Shakespeare's grave in Holy Trinity Church – one of the most beautiful parish churches in England. It is on the stage that Shakespeare is brought to life and nowhere more so than at a performance by the world's leading classical theatre company, the Royal Shakespeare Company.

[1] poet
[2] two features of Tudor houses
[3] is tucked away

59

Reviewing what's been learnt

In this section you have:

- Developed your skills as active, critical readers of various modern and contemporary texts about Shakespeare and his times.
- Developed your research skills, using ICT and books, to find out about witches in Shakespeare's time, and written up your research as an information leaflet.
- Reviewed the features of explanation texts, and written an explanation of how computers can help you with research.
- Written a descriptive text, adapting its style to a particular audience and purpose.
- Investigated the features of CD-ROMs and considered their effectiveness as research tools.
- Planned and written a tourist brochure as a group, together with an explanation of how you did this.
- Evaluated your skills in speaking and listening and in group discussion.

Now it's time to think about what things you have learnt from this section, and list the key points in your exercise book, using the following sentence starters to help you:

The key things I have learnt about writing in this section are ...

I now understand more about ...

When presenting ideas, I now know ...

Some of the vocabulary I now feel more confident about using is ...

The words I have learnt to spell are ...

The things I found most difficult were ...

The things I think I did best were ...

I now feel more confident about ...

My targets to improve my work are: (include reading, writing, spelling, speaking and listening)

-
-
-
-
-
-

Persuade, argue, advise

Introduction

Wanting others to share our beliefs and opinions is a natural part of being human. We use a range of techniques to argue a point of view or give advice, and we practise the art of persuasion almost before we can talk. In this section you will be looking at aspects of persuasion, argument and advice within the context of two very particular types of writing – poetry and reportage. Although very different in terms of form, both poetry and reportage serve a similar purpose: they tell us more about the world and the lives of other people by giving us an intimate personal perspective.

Whether you see poetry as fun, a challenge or a window of the soul, it has been a popular form of expression for thousands of years, long before the first novel was written. Every culture in the world has its own treasure chest of poetry. In this section you will be learning about different forms of poetry and writing some yourself.

We can read history books and newspapers to tell us what has happened, and is happening, in the world, but if you really want to know what it was like to be there, to live through a big event such as a war or a protest, then reportage gives you that insight. Reportage consists of accounts, letters and diaries, written sometimes by journalists sent to record events and sometimes by ordinary people caught up in those events. By being able to record their impressions they leave a rich legacy for future generations to learn from.

Key aims

In this section you will:
- Develop your understanding of, and skill in using, the devices that writers employ to make texts persuade, argue or advise.
- Experiment yourselves with writing in different forms and styles.

Inciting rhyme to riot

Aims

On these two pages you will:

- Analyse the structure and sound effects of a poem and how these are used to convey meaning.
- Consider the effect of using figurative language in poetry.
- Understand how meanings are conveyed in different ways, including through the use of irony.
- Recognize how a poem can reflect the culture and values of the person who wrote it.

Starter *as a group*

This lesson you will be analysing the poem 'Listen Mr Oxford Don' by John Agard (page 63). Your teacher will assign one of the verses to your group.

1 Read it out loud in your group and listen to the sound effects.
2 Decide what the **rhythm** of the verse is by listening to the beats of the lines and working out the **metre**.
3 Prepare a reading of your verse to perform to the rest of the class. Use the voices in your group – you could all read it together, or you could add interest by varying the number of voices speaking at any one time.

After each group has performed their verse, decide whether Agard has used the same rhythm throughout the poem.

Introduction *in pairs*

1 As you read the poem, you probably noticed that Agard has used lots of different sound effects which add to the rhythm and movement of the poem. Choose the lines that you think are the most effective and identify the elements that you think make it effective. You should consider:
- Alliteration
- Assonance
- Repetition
- Rhyme
- Rhythm.
2 This poem has been written to be spoken and performed. What effect does this have on the rhythm and sound effects of the poem?

Be prepared to feed back your ideas to the class.

Development *as a group*

In groups, examine the poem in more detail, using the questions on **Worksheet 50** as the basis for your discussion. Make notes on each question on the worksheet and be prepared to feed back your answers.

metre the way in which words and syllables are arranged in poetry or music to create a regular rhythm
rhythm a regular pattern of sound created by the choice and arrangement of words, especially in verse. The pattern is made by the alternation of light and heavy beats (or stresses).

Consider the **irony** in Agard's poem.

When, in the first verse, Agard says that he is a 'simple immigrant' he is speaking ironically.

- Why do you think this is ironic? What evidence can you find in the rest of the poem that proves he is far from 'simple'?
- Find another example of irony in the poem.
- Why do you think Agard uses irony to make his points?

irony a type of humour in which words are used to imply the opposite of what they normally mean

Plenary

Using your whiteboard or a piece of paper, write down three methods that John Agard has used in his poem to express his meaning.

John Agard was born in Guyana in 1949. He moved to Britain in 1977. He is a performance poet, actor, jazz performer and a lecturer at the Commonwealth Institute. His poems are often fun, but there is always a serious meaning hidden just beneath the surface.

Listen Mr Oxford Don

Me not no Oxford don[1]
me a simple immigrant
from Clapham Common[2]
I didn't graduate
I immigrate

But listen Mr Oxford don
I'm a man on de run
and a man on de run
is a dangerous one

I ent have no gun
I ent have no knife
but mugging de Queen's English[3]
is the story of my life

I don't need no axe
to split/up yu syntax
I don't need no hammer
to mash/up yu grammar

I warning you Mr Oxford don
I'm a wanted man
and a wanted man
is a dangerous one

Dem accuse me of assault
on de Oxford dictionary/
imagine a concise peaceful man like me/
dem want me serve time
for inciting rhyme to riot
but I tekking it quiet
down here in Clapham Common

I'm not a violent man Mr Oxford don
I only armed wit mih human breath
but human breath
is a dangerous weapon

So mek dem send one big word after me
I ent serving no jail sentence
I slashing suffix in self-defence
I bashing future wit present tense
and if necessary
I making de Queen's English accessory[4]/to my offence

John Agard

[1] a university teacher, in this case at Oxford University
[2] an area of south London
[3] Standard English
[4] a legal term describing the person who incites someone to commit a crime

Poems that offer advice

Aims

On these two pages you will:

- Analyse how poems may be structured in different ways.
- Explore the use of stylistic techniques such as repetition and imagery in poems.
- Understand the different choices that poets make by comparing two poems that give advice.

Starter  in pairs

Benjamin Zephaniah also uses a particular rhythm and **rhyme scheme** to emphasize the message of his poem 'City Friends Advice' (page 65). Listen as your teacher reads the poem to you and then, in pairs, answer the questions on **Worksheet 51**.

Be prepared to feed back your ideas to the class.

rhyme scheme the way rhyming words are organized in a poem. When writing out a rhyme scheme you usually use different letters for each line, but the same letter if two lines rhyme. For example, '… cars/… knives/… guns/… lives' has the rhyme scheme ABCB.

Introduction as a class

When poets start to write a poem they have several choices to make, not only about what they want to say but also about how their message should be expressed. Some poets choose to structure their poems in a particularly traditional way, such as a sonnet. Other poets, such as Zephaniah, choose to create verses with their own rhythm and/or rhyme scheme.

You may also have come across poems that have no formal structure at all – no rhyme or regular rhythm, no verses, no capital letters at the beginning of every line, sometimes even no punctuation. These poems, written in what is called **free verse**, became very popular in the twentieth century. Isobel Thrilling's poem 'Advice to a Teenage Daughter' (page 65) is a good example of a poem written in free verse.

Listen as your teacher reads the poem to you.

 in pairs

Discuss and make notes on the questions on **Worksheet 52**.

Be prepared to feed back your ideas to the class.

free verse verse that has neither rhyme nor a regular rhythm

Development in pairs

Both these poems are offering advice. What similarities and differences can you find between them? In pairs, fill in the grid on **Worksheet 53** to help you to compare the two poems, considering the following features in particular:

- Structure
- Style: the effect of language, repetition, imagery and figurative language
- Tone: use of humour and irony
- Advice offered.

Plenary

- If you prefer 'City Friends Advice', write down three ways in which you think rhyme and rhythm contribute to the meaning and effect of a poem.
- If you prefer 'Advice to a Teenage Daughter', write down three ways in which you think the absence of rhyme and rhythm contribute to the meaning and effect of a poem.

Be prepared to share your views.

homework

Write a comparison of the two poems for homework. Use your comparison grid (**Worksheet 53**) to help you structure your answer.

! **Remember** to read your work carefully, improve it if necessary and write a brief comment on how well you think you have completed the task.

City Friends Advice

Beware of the cars
And beware of the knives,
Beware of the guns
And take care of your lives,
Beware of all those
That are out very late,
Even in daytime
Beware of your mate.

Beware of the dogs
For they are highly trained,
Beware of the humans
For they are not tamed,
Beware of all food
That may have a bad taste,
Beware
On your plate could be
Chemical waste.

Beware of the preacher
For he wants your voice,
If you want to survive
You will have no choice,
Beware of yourself
And you do not know me,
Just enjoy your stay
In this modern city.

Benjamin Zephaniah

Advice to a Teenage Daughter

You have found a new war-game
called Love.
Here on your dressing-table
stand arrayed
brave ranks of lipsticks
brandishing
swords of cherry pink and flame.
Behold the miniature armies
of little jars,
packed with the scented
dynamite of flowers.
See the dreaded tweezers;
tiny pots
of manufactured moonlight,
stick-on stars.
Beware my sweet;
conquest may seem easy
but you can't compete with football,
motor cycles, cars,
cricket, computer-games,
or a plate of chips.

Isobel Thrilling

Benjamin Zephaniah (born 1958) is a writer, actor and TV and radio presenter. His first book of poetry, *Pen Rhythm*, was published when he was 22.

Isobel Thrilling (born 1935) has published three volumes of poetry, much of it based around the theme of science. Her latest work is *The Chemistry of Angels*.

Poems that persuade

Aims

On these two pages you will:

- Explore how a text follows or adapts a traditional form.
- Recognize irony in a poem and explore how it is conveyed.
- Explore how poets write in different narrative voices.
- Experiment with writing poetry in different forms and styles.

Starter  as a group

Listen as your teacher reads you the poem 'Lullaby' by Rosemary Norman (**Worksheet 54**). Then, in groups, discuss the questions below. You may like to use your copy of the poem to make notes.

Be prepared to feed back your answers.

1 Examine and comment on the structure of the poem. Think about:

- The number of lines in the verses
- The use of repetition
- Rhythm
- Rhyme.

   What type of poem is this?

2 What do you notice about the order of things that the 'baby' talks about as they appear in the poem? Why do you think the poet has done this?

3 How and why does the baby persuade the mother to relax and 'go to sleep'? If you were the mother would you be persuaded?

4 This poem is called 'Lullaby'. Traditionally a lullaby is a soothing song sung by adults to help children to sleep; what features does this poem share with a lullaby? How does it also contrast with what you would ordinarily expect from a lullaby?

5 What effect do the last two lines in the poem create? Why do you think the poet has chosen to end her poem in this way?

Introduction as a group

Although many poems are written from a very personal perspective, it is important to remember that poets, like novelists, often write in voices other than their own. This allows them to put forward different viewpoints.

The voice of the poem that you have just read in the starter activity is that of a baby lulling their mother to sleep. The second poem you are going to study today, also by Benjamin Zephaniah, is written from the perspective of an 'old timer'.

Listen as your teacher reads you the poem 'The Wise Old Timer' on page 67. In groups, discuss the questions on the poem on **Worksheet 55**. Remember to record your responses and be ready to feed back your ideas to the class.

Development on your own

It is now your turn to experiment with writing poetry. You are probably very familiar with the views and expressions used in 'The Wise Old Timer'. Your task is to write a poem from your parent's perspective, addressed directly to you, which expresses some of these views and includes some of the clichés you listed for the activity in the introduction. Your poem should:

- Have a regular structure of verses, each with six lines
- Have a clear rhythm
- Have a rhyme scheme.

Use **Worksheet 56** to help you plan your poem.

Plenary

Two people from the class will be asked to read out the start of their poems. Do they have a clear rhythm?

homework

Write a reply to the poem you have written in class, this time from your own perspective and giving your own point of view. This poem should be written in free verse, so it doesn't have to have any rhythm, rhyme or set structure.

! **Remember** to read your work carefully, improve it if necessary and write a brief comment on how well you think you have completed the task.

The Wise Old Timer

When I was your age
Kids were different
Only spoke when spoken to
Only swore when alone,
We went to school
Then to work
All in a day,
Kids nowadays don't understand.

When I was your age
Kids were kids,
We could not
Ask for more,
Choose our meals,
Debate with parents
Enter without knocking,
Kids nowadays don't behave.

When I was your age
I was working the pit
Fighting the war
With coal
And the Germans,
To make sure kids nowadays
Get freedom
Nuclear power
And the pill,
When I was your age
I weren't like you.

Kids now talk about
Their rights
Their space
Their music
Their interests
Their problems
They cry aloud
They have
Their own ideas
They even
Use the phone,
Meat used to be a luxury
Now I see tiny vegetarians,
Every bloody where.
We made our toys
Now they want money,
We went to the cinema
They have cameras,
What next I ask
What next.

When we were told to do
We done,
And when we did,
We did it properly,
They do anything now,
It's called expression,
When we were told to
We did,
We did not
Ask why.
Kids nowadays
Get away with murder.

When I was your age
Kids were different,
Roses were red
Violets were blue
Poor but fed
We struggled too,
Baths were special
Sweets were treats
Homework was done
And he who wore trousers
Ruled.
Who wears the trousers now?

When you are my age
You'll see kids in a different light
And you'll understand
How kids are different now,
Kids are not like kids anymore,
They're like little Human Beings.

Benjamin Zephaniah

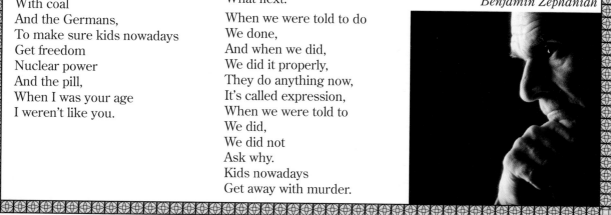

Landscapes of the mind

Aims

On these two pages you will:

- Explore the way in which poets use landscapes to express issues of both personal and general significance.

- Recognize how texts reflect the culture in which they were produced.

- Examine the poetic features of writing in free verse.

- Write a poem about a landscape that relates to your own experiences.

Starter

Listen as your teacher reads Derek Walcott's poem 'Midsummer, Tobago' to you, and then answer the questions below in pairs.

1 What type of poem is this? Make a list of the poetic features that you recognize from your earlier work on poetry.

2 Imagine, or make a quick sketch of, the scene that the poem describes in the first five lines of the poem. Talk about how the poet has created this picture in your mind.

3 What do you think the poet means when he says, 'Days I have held,/ days I have lost'?

4 Explain the image created by the figurative language used in the last two lines of the poem, 'days that outgrow, like daughters,/ my harbouring arms'.

5 What do you think is the overall message of the poem?

Be prepared to feed back your ideas to the class.

Introduction *as a group*

In his poem 'In the Desert' (**Worksheet 57**), Zulfikar Ghose also creates a landscape for his readers to picture in their minds. Like Derek Walcott's island world, this landscape expresses something significant about the poet's own life, as well as something more general about human experience.

Listen as your teacher reads you 'In the Desert'. Then, in groups, discuss the following questions.

Midsummer, Tobago[1]

Broad sun-stoned beaches.

White heat.
A green river.

A bridge,
scorched yellow palms

from the summer-sleeping house
drowsing through August.

Days I have held,
days I have lost,

days that outgrow, like daughters,
my harbouring arms.

[1] an island in the Caribbean

Derek Walcott was born on the Caribbean island of St Lucia in 1930. He has written many plays, though he is perhaps more famous now for his poetry, which often explores the inter-relationship between the many different cultures of the Caribbean people. In 1992 he was awarded the Nobel Prize for Literature.

1   Describe the landscape that the train travels through on its journey to Quetta.

2   As a young boy Ghose is struck by the emptiness of the desert. Find two quotations from the poem that reflect this feeling.

3   In the final **stanza** Ghose says that he still feels as if he is 'searching the horizon for plants'. What do you think this image of the plants actually means?

4   What aspects of our own lives could be called 'a desert'?

Be prepared to feed back your ideas to the class.

stanza a verse

Development on your own

Now you are going to write a poem about a landscape that relates to your own experience. First of all, brainstorm ideas by using **Worksheet 58**: these ideas will help you plan your poem.

●   Using the model of Norman and Zephaniah's poems in the last lesson, write in a voice that is not quite your own, as if you were forty years older, looking back at the place you describe. How might the place and your feelings towards it have changed?

●   Following the examples of Walcott and Ghose in this lesson, write in free verse. This will give you the advantage of not having to use words that fit a particular rhythm or rhyme scheme.

●   You will need to make decisions about the structure of your poem. Consider the questions on the noticeboard above.

Writing in free verse

Will every line begin with a capital letter? Sometimes poets have a capital letter at the start of every line (e.g. Zephaniah); others only have capital letters where a real sentence begins (e.g. Ghose).

Will you use punctuation or not? Some poets choose not to have any punctuation in their poems. The reader has to decide where it should be, which sometimes makes the poems rather challenging to read.

Will there be stanzas or no breaks at all? Walcott has stanzas with no regular pattern, Ghose has chosen four-line stanzas, but you could choose to have no breaks in your poem at all.

How long will your lines be? You can vary the length from one word to several, but make sure that you think about the structure and pattern of your poem. Never start a new line in poetry just because you have come to the edge of the page!

What type of poetic effects will you use? As your poem is free verse it will not be necessary to use rhyme or a regular rhythm, but you should try to use other stylistic features, such as sound effects (e.g. assonance and alliteration) and figurative language (e.g. similes and metaphors).

Plenary

Using your whiteboard or a piece of paper, jot down three choices that you have made about the structure of your poem.

Be prepared to share your choices with the rest of the class.

homework

Write your landscape poem for homework.

!   **Remember** to read your work carefully, improve it if necessary and write a brief comment on how well you think you have completed the task.

Persuading your teacher

Aims

On these two pages you will:
- Reflect on what you have learnt about poetry in this section.
- Present a case persuasively by selecting evidence and making comparisons.
- Think about different ways of linking paragraphs to improve the coherence and cohesion of your writing.

Starter

Later in this lesson you will be writing a text that attempts to persuade the reader of your point of view. First, in pairs, remind each other of the main structure and language features of texts that persuade.

Be prepared to feed back your ideas to the class.

Linking paragraphs with a variety of connectives or connecting phrases is one feature of texts that persuade. This can strengthen the argument of a text in two main ways:
- By linking its ideas in a logical way to improve its **coherence**
- By signposting the structure to improve its **cohesion**.

coherence the underlying logic and consistency of a text. In a coherent text the ideas expressed should be relevant to one another so that the reader can follow the meaning.

cohesion the way in which the parts of a text fit together. This is often signposted by grammatical features such as connectives.

Each group will be given 18 different connectives on cards (**Worksheet 59**). Sort them into the six categories below:
- ***Addition*** – to add a new point.
- ***Opposition*** – to qualify your statement.
- ***Reinforcing*** – to add strength to an existing point.
- ***Explaining*** – to give an example or explanation.
- ***Listing*** – to signpost a list of features or points.
- ***Referring back*** – to remind the reader of an earlier point.

Be prepared to feed back to the class.

Introduction as a group

1 Reflecting on what you have learnt about poetry so far, put together a list of five features that you think a good poem should display. Be prepared to feed back your list to the class.

2 On your own, use your list as criteria to help you decide which is the best of all the poems that you have studied in this section. The poem doesn't have to match your criteria exactly, but if it doesn't, it would be interesting to consider why you prefer it nevertheless.

3 Each member of the group now has one minute to tell the others why the poem they have chosen is the best.

Development *on your own*

Your task is to persuade your teacher that your chosen poem is the best of all those that you have studied in this section. Argue your case by analysing your poem and comparing it with others. Use what you have learnt about poetry as supporting evidence.

Remember that to be convincing you will need to make your writing persuasive. This means thinking about the strength of your language as well as the strength of your argument.

Use **Worksheet 60** to help you to plan your essay (you will write the essay for homework). Think about the following points when filling in the worksheet:

My reasons for choosing this poem.

Talk about your personal reactions and responses to this poem, how you can relate to it – perhaps through the subject matter, the poem's voice or its humour. Try not to mention things in too much detail that will be dealt with in separate paragraphs later on.

The special features of this poem which make it a pleasure to read.

Include here points about structure, use of figurative language, rhyme, rhythm and expression.

The message of the poem.

What does the poem say that you think is interesting, entertaining or important?

How it compares with other poems.

Mention two or three other poems that you might have considered and the reasons why you rejected them in favour of your final choice. (This does not mean saying the others are no good; it means pointing out why you think they are not quite as good as your best poem.) Make direct comparisons with the points that you have made about your own poem.

How to sum up your argument.

A concluding paragraph should sum up your argument in an effective way.

Plenary

Using your whiteboard or a piece of paper, write down three of the most important ingredients of a successful poem.

Be prepared to share your list with the rest of the class.

homework

Write the essay that you have planned, persuading your teacher that your chosen poem is the best.

> **!** **Remember**
>
> - Your essay should show the structure and language features of texts that persuade. Above all, use connectives to link your paragraphs in a logical and coherent way.
> - Read your work carefully, asking yourself if you would be persuaded. Improve it if necessary and write a brief comment on how well you think you have completed the task.

I was there

Aims

On these two pages you will:
- Develop an understanding of what reportage is.
- Think about what makes good reportage writing.
- Use mnemonics to help you to remember the spelling of particular words.

Starter as a class

Mnemonics are little phrases or sentences that help you to remember things. Here are some examples:

environment
there is **iron** in the envi**ron**ment

friend
the end of fri**end** is **end**

fulfil
knock the l out of full and fill

necessary
it is necessary to have one **c**ollar and two **s**ocks

stationery
envelopes are station**e**ry

Over the years you will probably have developed your own mnemonics to help you to spell particular words. Now is the time to share them.

1 On a separate sheet of paper write your word and the mnemonic that goes with it.

2 When all your class's mnemonics are complete, display them round the room for others to read. Learn any new ones which you think will be useful.

3 If you can't think of one of your own, try devising a useful and memorable phrase that will help you to distinguish between combinations like:
   – 'there', 'they're' and 'their'
   – 'council' and 'counsel'
   – 'accept' and 'except'
   – 'principal' and 'principle'.
   Or invent mnemonics for the following words:
   – 'business'
   – 'success'
   – 'opinion'.

Introduction as a class

Reportage describes a type of writing that you can find in many different places, including newspapers, diaries, letters, travelogues and on the radio. It usually involves an eye-witness account of a particular event which is of interest to other people.

You are going to start by studying three examples of reportage, reprinted here and on **Worksheet 61**. Listen as your teacher reads the extracts to you and then discuss the following questions:

1 Who is 'speaking' in each case?

2 Where would the text have appeared originally?

3 How are these texts different from autobiography?

4 What features do they have in common?

September 2, 1666

So I made myself ready and walked to the Tower[1] and got up upon one of the high places. There I did see the houses at the end of the bridge all on fire, and an infinite great fire on this and the other side of the bridge ... So down I went with my heart full of trouble to the Lieutenant of the Tower, who told me that the fire had begun this morning in the King's baker's house in Pudding Lane, and that it had burned down St Magnes Church and most of Fish Street already. So I went down to the water-side, and there got a boat, from which I saw a lamentable fire. Poor Michell's house was already burned, and the fire running further, so that it got as far as the Steele-yard while I was there. Everybody was endeavouring to remove their goods, flinging them into the river, or into lighters[2] that lay off. Some poor people were staying in their houses until the fire touched them, and then running into boats, or clambering from one pair of stairs by the water-side to another. And the poor pigeons were unwilling to leave their houses, but hovered about the windows and balconies, till they burned their wings, and fell down.

And so I stayed, and in an hour's time saw the fire rage every way, and nobody to my sight endeavouring to quench it, but instead removing their goods and leaving all to the fire.

Samuel Pepys

[1] *Tower of London*   [2] *boats for carrying goods*

Development *in pairs*

In pairs, work through the following questions and use the grid on **Worksheet 62** to record your answers.

1 The heading for these pages is 'I was there'. For each extract write down which parts of the extract gave you the impression of being there. When you have done this, highlight the extract that gives you the strongest feeling of 'being there'.

2 Do you think any of these writers has a point to make? Why were they writing in the first place?

3 The Pepys extract is a diary, the one from Mayhew is a **transcript** of a conversation and Bradberry's is a piece of journalism. Write down your observations on how this affects the way the extracts are organized.

Samuel Pepys (1633–1703) was Naval Secretary in the reign of Charles II. His diary, which he began in 1660, provides a fascinating first-hand account of life in London in the 1660s.

transcript a written version of something that is spoken

Plenary

As a class, decide which of these three extracts you thought was best at giving you an impression of 'being there'. Use evidence from your grid to support your view.

Reportage with attitude

Aims

On these two pages you will:

- Learn how to recognize bias in reportage.
- Write your own account of an event and compare it with an account written by your partner.

Starter

Reportage often deals with important public events which are recounted by individuals who were there at the time. Sometimes reportage is a straight factual account of the events, but often it is influenced by the attitudes of the person who wrote it and therefore written from the writer's point of view. This can mean that the account is **biased**.

> **biased** unfairly presented to favour one point of view over another

in pairs

To help you explore this idea further, imagine that there has been an anti-GM foods protest march in London. How will the different people involved respond to it? Each of the people listed below will have had different attitudes to the event. Think about what they might have said about the protest and write a quote for two of these people to create a speech card.

- Anti-GM foods protester
- A police officer on crowd control duty
- A government minister
- A journalist
- A motorist held up by the march
- A tourist

 as a class

1 Put each of your speech cards in a pile. One person from each pair should come up and read one of the speech cards out to the rest of the class, using the tone and expression appropriate to the quote.

2 Imagine that all these people wrote accounts of the march. In what ways are their accounts likely to be biased, and why?

Introduction **as a class**

Read the account of the execution in 1793 of King Louis XVI of France (page 75). It was written by an Irish priest, the Abbé Edgworth, who travelled with the king on his final journey to the scaffold.

as a group

Discuss and make notes on the following questions. Be prepared to feed back your answers to the rest of the class.

1 How does the Abbé describe the king? What effect does this have on the reader's attitude to the events?

2 What is the Abbé's attitude towards King Louis and what is about to happen? Use evidence from the text to support your answer.

3 The Abbé often quotes the king (and others). What is the effect of this?

4 Do you think that this is a reliable account of an historical event? Give reasons for your answer.

As soon as the king got out of the coach, three of the executioners surrounded him, and tried to remove his outer garments. He pushed them away with dignity, and took off his coat himself. He also took off his collar and his shirt, and made himself ready with his own hands. The executioners, disconnected[1] for a moment by the king's proud bearing,[2] recovered themselves and surrounded him again in order to bind his hands.

'What are you doing?' said the king, quickly drawing his hands back.

'Binding your hands,' answered one of them.

'Binding me!' said the king in a voice of indignation. 'Never! Do what you have been ordered, but you shall never bind me.'

The executioners insisted; they spoke more loudly, and seemed about to call for help to force the king to obey.

This was the most agonising moment of this terrible morning; one minute more, and the best of kings would have received an outrage a thousand times worse than death, by the violence that they were about to use towards him. He appeared to fear this himself, and turning his head, seemed to ask my advice. At first I remained silent, but when he continued to look at me, I said, with tears in my eyes, 'Sire, in this new outrage I see one last resemblance between Your Majesty and the God Who is about to be your reward.'

At these words he raised his eyes to heaven with an expression of unutterable[3] sadness. 'Surely,' he replied, 'it needs nothing less than His example to make me submit to such an insult.' Then, turning to the executioners: 'Do what you will; I will drink the cup,[4] even to the dregs.'

The steps of the scaffold were extremely steep. The king was obliged to lean on my arm, and from the difficulty they caused him, I feared that his courage was beginning to wane;[5] but what was my astonishment when, arrived at the top, he let go of me, crossed the scaffold with a firm step, silenced with a glance the fifteen or twenty drummers who had been placed directly opposite, and in a voice so loud that it could be heard as far away as the Font Tournant, pronounced these unforgettable words: 'I die innocent of all the crimes with which I am charged. I forgive those who are guilty of my death, and I pray God that the blood which you are about to shed may never be required of France.'

Development *in pairs*

Working with a partner, think of an interesting experience you have shared – it might be a sports event or a pop concert. Once you have agreed on the experience, work on your own to write as vivid an account of the experience as possible.

When you have finished, compare your writing. Do you both mention the same facts? Are the events told in the same order? Do you share the same views and opinions about what happened?

Be prepared to share with the class what you have discovered.

[1] taken aback
[2] behaviour
[3] unspeakable
[4] I will accept my fate
[5] fade away

Plenary

Name three ways that you would use to assess whether an account is biased.

Do you think it matters that some reportage is biased?

Using reportage as a source

Aims

On these two pages you will:

- Explore how reportage can be used as a source of information about historical events.
- Develop your skills in varying sentence constructions in your own writing.

Starter  in pairs

One of the signs of good writing is its ability to engage its readers' interest.

1 In the table on **Worksheet 63** are five things that make writing interesting. Put a number by each one to show how important you think it is (1 = of greatest importance, 5 = of least importance). Then compare your view with a partner's and, after discussion, come up with an agreed rank order of the factors that make writing interesting. Put this in the final column.

2 As you have seen in previous sections of this book, sentence variety doesn't just happen: it's something you need to think about as you write, and it should be high on the list of things that you think about when you re-draft your work.

With a partner, read the paragraph on **Worksheet 63**, which has been written using a very unimaginative sentence structure. Rewrite it in the space provided to make it more interesting. Think about:

- The length of the sentences you will use

- The type of sentences you will include, such as simple, complex or compound
- The order of the clauses within the sentences.

When you have completed your paragraph, compare it with another pair's.

> **simple sentence** a sentence containing only one clause: 'Salman took the bus.'

Introduction

Most reportage is biased in some way because it is based on a single point of view. It is therefore important to think about who has written the piece of reportage and why they have written their account.

Whether you mind about the bias depends on your reason for reading. If you want to get a vivid personal impression, then someone's diary is probably better than any number of history books. If you are trying to understand an important or interesting event, then you will need to read more than one account. Historians often use a variety of sources to help them to establish a clear picture of an important historical event or character.

in pairs

The ocean liner *Titanic* struck an iceberg in the north Atlantic and sank on 15 April 1912. Over 1500 people drowned; the disaster shocked the world. The extracts on **Worksheet 64** consist of two eyewitness accounts of how the ship went down. Listen as your teacher reads you the accounts,

and then discuss the following
questions in pairs.

1 From what point of view is each
   account written?

2 Do the accounts focus on exactly
   the same events? If not, why not?

3 Which account gives the more
   detailed description of events?

4 Is one account more factual than
   the other? Is one more emotive?

5 Do you think these are accurate
   accounts of what happened?

Development on your own

The two pieces of reportage that you
have read are important eyewitness
accounts of a well-known historical
event. An historian would call them
'primary sources'. Because individual
experiences are different, each primary
source will have a different point of
view, or perspective, of events. This
makes sources like these invaluable to
writers such as historians and
journalists, as they piece together what
really happened in order to write their
more objective accounts.

Your task is to write a short account
of the sinking of the *Titanic* from a
more objective perspective. First of
all, use **Worksheet 65** to help you
examine the extracts for information
so that you can plan this account.
Remember to quote from the extracts,
just as an historian would quote from
primary sources, to back up your
description with evidence.

Plenary

Identify three key differences
between reportage and objective
narrative accounts.

homework

Write your account of the sinking of
the *Titanic* for homework.

> **!** **Remember** to make your sentence
> structure interesting and varied (think
> about the work you did in the starter
> activity). Read your work carefully, improve
> it if necessary and write a brief comment
> on how well you think you have completed
> the task.

Sequencing in reportage texts

Aims

On these two pages you will:

- Examine the way reportage texts are structured and explore how events can be sequenced to create interest.
- Write advice to Year 8 students on sequencing their own writing.
- Experiment with sequencing by writing your own piece of reportage.
- Develop your understanding of spelling patterns by exploring word roots.

Starter in pairs

As many words share the same root, one way of helping to spell words is to think about their roots. To help you to understand this further, complete the activity on **Worksheet 66** with a partner.

Introduction as a class

Most reportage has an overall linear structure: it begins at the beginning and works its way through to the end. However, to follow this plan rigidly would be very dull; authors like to look backwards or forwards from time to time.

Think about the reasons why authors may wish to break the chronological sequence of their writing. Here are some ideas to start you off:

- To fill in background detail
- To anticipate a forthcoming event.

In the passage on **Worksheet 67**, the journalist Alistair Cooke writes about the moment in 1967 when Muhammad Ali, formerly known as Cassius Clay, became the undisputed heavyweight boxing champion of the world. Read the passage as a class.

in pairs

Work through the following activities in pairs.

1   On a piece of paper, list the order of events in Alistair Cooke's account exactly as he narrates them.

2   Draw a timeline across another piece of paper. Mark on your line the sequence of events as they would actually have happened.

3   Compare the order of events you have written down with the order in the passage.

4   Discuss why you think Alistair Cooke did not present the fight in chronological order.

Development *on your own*

Look at the timeline of events given below, in which your favourite football team wins an important match.

Your task is to write a paragraph of advice to Year 8 students on how to sequence these events in an interesting and exciting way. Think about the work you did in the introduction activity and use **Worksheet 68** to plan your work. Your advice should outline the possible approaches that students could take to the writing task.

Plenary

- Feed back your advice to the class.
- Discuss whether 'start at the beginning and work your way through to the end' is a good piece of advice for writers or not.

homework

Using the advice you created in the development activity, write an interesting account of the football match, including details and descriptions where relevant.

> **!** **Remember** that this should be a piece of reportage, like Alistair Cooke's account, not a straightforward commentary on the match. Read your work carefully, improve it if necessary and write a brief comment on how well you think you have completed the task.

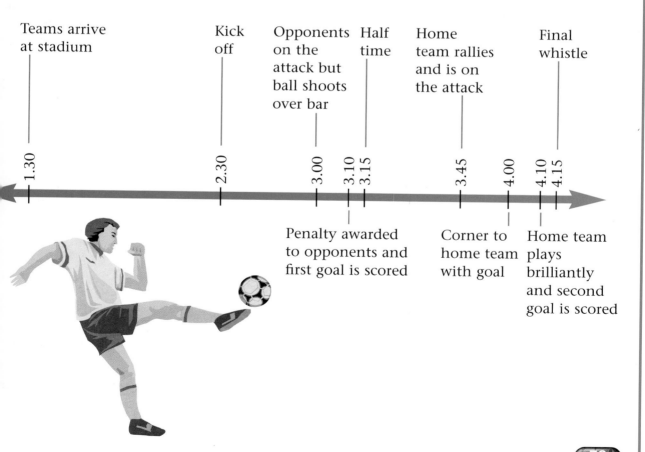

Teams arrive at stadium — 1.30

Kick off — 2.30

Opponents on the attack but ball shoots over bar — 3.00

Penalty awarded to opponents and first goal is scored — 3.10

Half time — 3.15

Home team rallies and is on the attack — 3.45

Corner to home team with goal — 4.00

Final whistle — 4.10

Home team plays brilliantly and second goal is scored — 4.15

Opinion pieces

Aims

On these two pages you will:
- Explore how reporting personal experiences can enhance an argument.
- Write an opinion piece which presents an argument.
- Practise spelling words which do not conform to regular patterns.

Starter  in pairs

Listen as your teacher reads the following poem to you.

The Chaos

Dearest *creature* in *creation*,
Studying English pronunciation,
I will teach you in my verse
Sounds like *corpse*, *corps*, *horse* and *worse*.
5 I will keep you, *Susy*, *busy*,
Make your *head* with *heat* grow dizzy.
Tear in eye your dress you'll *tear*.
So shall I! Oh, hear my *prayer*.
Pray, console your loving poet,
10 Make my coat look *new*, dear, *sew* it!
Just compare *heart*, *beard* and *heard*,
Dies and *diet*, *lord* and *word*,
Sword and *sward*, *retain* and *Britain*.
(Mind the latter, how it's written!)
15 Now I surely will not *plague* you
With such words as *vague* and *ague*,
But be careful how you speak:
Say *break*, *steak*, but *bleak* and *streak*;
Cloven, *oven*; *how* and *low*;
20 *Script*, *receipt*; *show*, *poem*, *toe*.

Billet does not rhyme with *ballet*,
Bouquet, *wallet*, *mallet*, *chalet*;
Blood and *flood* are not like *food*,
Nor is *mould* like *should* and *would*.
25 *Viscous*, *viscount*; *load* and *broad*;
Toward, to *forward*, to *reward*.
And your pronunciation's OK
When you correctly say *croquet*;
Rounded, *wounded*; *grieve* and *sieve*;
30 *Friend* and *fiend*; *alive* and *live*.
River, *rival*; *tomb*, *bomb*, *comb*;
Doll and *roll* and *some* and *home*.
Stranger does not rhyme with *anger*,
Neither does *devour* with *clangour*.
35 *Soul* but *foul*; and *gaunt* but *aunt*;
Font, *front*, *wont*; *want*, *grand* and *grant*;
Shoes, *goes*, *does*. Now first say *finger*,
And then *singer*, *ginger*, *linger*;
Real, *zeal*; *mauve*, *gauze* and *gauge*;
40 *Marriage*, *foliage*, *mirage*, *age*.

Charivarius (G. N. Trenité)

Your teacher will give each pair three or four groups of words that the author has used. Say them to each other, and check that you have got the pronunciation right. Then combine with another pair, and read out your words to test their spelling. (They will do the same with you, of course.)

Write any words you misspelt in your spelling log.

Introduction *as a class*

Reporting personal experiences can provide a strong backbone to pieces of writing that are intended to persuade, argue or advise.

To examine this idea more closely read the **opinion piece** 'Welcome them' on **Worksheet 69** and then discuss the following questions.

1 Look at the first three paragraphs of the article:

- Why do you think Julia Neuberger chose to begin her article with her own personal experience?
- How do her experiences affect her opinions on asylum seekers?
- How do her experiences affect your view of asylum seekers?

2 Look at the final two paragraphs of the article. Use the grid on **Worksheet 70** to help you to record all the techniques Neuberger uses at the end of this extract to argue her point of view.

3 How does what we have read and understood at the beginning of the article affect how we respond to her arguments against the asylum bill?

opinion piece an article in a newspaper which presents a personal view on an important issue

Development *on your own*

Imagine you are a journalist. You have been asked to write an opinion piece for a national newspaper about an issue of importance to you, for example animal cruelty or teenage drinking.

Use Julia Neuberger's article as a model for your own writing by starting with an account of your personal experience of the issue. For example:

- When have you seen animals suffering? What exactly happened and how did that make you feel?
- When have you experienced the effects of drinking too much?

When you have done this, use this experience to put forward an argument expressing a particular point of view on the issue. For example:

- There should be tougher penalties for those who are cruel to animals.
- There should be stricter controls on under-age drinking.

Draft your opinion piece, using the techniques of persuasive writing that you know. Think about the techniques that Neuberger used in her article.

Plenary

Listen while one or two people present their arguments to the class, and discuss the key points that you think make their arguments effective.

 homework

Produce a final draft of your article for homework.

! **Remember** to read your work carefully, improve it if necessary and write a brief comment on how well you think you have completed the task.

Reviewing what's been learnt

Through your work in this section you have explored two significant types of writing: poetry and reportage. By studying the techniques that writers use to engage their readers' attention, and to persuade, argue and advise, you will have developed your own understanding and knowledge of how words can be made to work for you. Now you should be able to reflect on these skills in your own writing.

In poetry you have learnt to use rhythm and rhyme when you need to create an effect, but you also know that free verse can carry a strong message in the modern day world. Knowing that writing can be biased even when it does not appear to be is an important life skill: remember it and be aware. In addition you have also been able to focus on spelling and the rules which will help you to spell new words correctly and check the old favourites.

Now it's time to think about what things you have learnt from this section, and list the key points in your exercise book, using the following sentence starters to help you:

The key things I have learnt about writing in this section are ...

I now understand more about ...

When presenting ideas, I now know ...

Some of the vocabulary I now feel more confident about using is ...

The words I have learnt to spell are ...

The things I found most difficult were ...

The things I think I did best were ...

I now feel more confident about ...

My targets to improve my work are:
(include reading, writing, spelling, speaking and listening)

-
-
-
-
-
-

Analyse, review, comment

Introduction

This year you're going to focus your analysis, review and comment on two very different kinds of text: short stories written before the outbreak of the First World War, and media and moving image texts.

The First World War (1914–1918) was one of the most terrible events in modern history. The world changed so much and so quickly after the war that the conflict is often regarded as a dividing line between an old way of life and the modern world. In the field of communications, for example, if you take the face of a clock to represent how communications have changed in the last 2000 years, most of the change has taken place in the last two minutes.

The analysis, review and comment that you will do in this section, therefore, will focus on texts on both sides of this defining line in human history.

Key aims

In this section you will:

- Develop your understanding of why writers make particular choices for different audiences and purposes, as well as developing your own ability to write analysis, review and comment effectively.

- Focus on how the news is presented in newspapers, on a website and on television, and consider what difference this makes to the news; then write and present a balanced analysis of how a story is covered in different newspapers.

Selecting the right words

Saki (1870–1916)

Aims

On these two pages you will:

- Develop your skills as critical readers, focusing on the author's perspective and playing text detective to consider why writers make particular choices.
- Analyse the structure of a story, identifying how key ideas are developed.
- Use a range of strategies to try to work out the meaning of unknown words.

Starter  as a group

Today you're going to read 'The Storyteller' by Saki but, before you focus on the whole story, you're going to read the opening paragraph on **Worksheet 71**. Some of the more difficult vocabulary has been highlighted. See if you can work out what all the highlighted words mean, without using a dictionary. Instead, use the following strategies:

- Context – use the rest of the sentence or passage to help you
- Syntax – work out what function the word plays in the sentence (e.g. is it a noun?)
- Etymology – think about the origin of the word
- Morphology – think about the roots and affixes that make up the word.

If possible, come up with an alternative word or phrase which would mean the same thing in this context, and note this down on **Worksheet 71**.

Be prepared to feed back your ideas, explaining what strategy you used to come to your conclusion.

Introduction as a class

In the Imagine section you looked at narrative perspective, focusing on first-person narrative. You can also write in the third person as if you are God and know everything that is going to happen to your characters (when you write like this, you are being an **omniscient author**). Another way of writing in the third person is to limit your viewpoint to that of the key character.

You've just read the opening of Saki's 'The Storyteller', which is written in the third person. Is he writing as an omniscient author or is he writing from the perspective of one of the characters? Does Saki seem to be close to the main characters or standing a long way back and examining them?

omniscient author a narrative voice in which an author writes from the godlike perspective of knowing everything about the characters' innermost thoughts and feelings as well as all the events of the story

Many of Saki's short stories centre on rather clever, if not always likeable, children who defeat unimaginative, overbearing adults. 'The Storyteller' is a perfect example. Your teacher will read you the story, pausing before the final section (**Worksheets 72a–c**). As your teacher reads the story, be prepared to join in discussion of the following questions:

- How has Saki constructed this story to make it effective? (How does it begin? How does it develop?)
- How has he selected words and constructed sentences to convey exactly the image, meaning or mood that he wanted?
- How does Saki prepare the reader for the ending of the story?
- Whose side are you increasingly on as this story develops?
- How has the writer achieved this?
- Does the writer want you to feel close to any of the characters or to stand back and laugh?
- How has the writer structured the story?

Help your teacher complete the structure flow chart below:

Introduction – Opening paragraph sets the scene and introduces the characters.

▼

Following dialogue – establishes personalities of the aunt, and the children and the bachelor's irritation.

▼

The aunt's story – establishes her lack of imagination or humour and her inability to engage an audience.

Development *in pairs*

In pairs, look at the section of the story from where the aunt attempts to tell the children a story to where the stranger begins to tell his story (lines 55–100). Highlight any words or phrases that you think convey mood or character in an imaginative way. Then fill in the grid on **Worksheet 73**, identifying the words and phrases you've selected and why you've selected them. Two examples have been completed for you:

Words and phrases that convey mood or character	Effect that the writer is trying to achieve
looked twice at her and once at the communication cord	The use of the numbers helps the reader imagine the bachelor's eye movements so that you can picture the scene as the atmosphere in the carriage worsens
listlessly	A good word to describe the extreme boredom of the children at the prospect of one of the aunt's stories

Plenary

Feed back your ideas and decide what are the key aspects of Saki's writing that make it effective.

Add Saki's 'The Storyteller' to your reading record.

Analysing colloquial language

Aims

On these two pages you will:

- Further develop your skills as critical readers, focusing on the author's perspective.
- Consider the differences between Standard English and dialect, using a note-taking grid to help you analyse the language used in a story.
- Think about ways of remembering how to spell tricky words from across the curriculum that don't fit standard patterns, including sounding out words.

Starter as a group

Look at the 20 words listed below. They are rather tricky to spell because they don't fit any regular patterns to help you with their pronunciation.

- In your groups, first practise sounding out these words so that you are sure of how to pronounce them.
- Now try to think of ways that might help you to spell them, for example a mnemonic like 'there's always **a rat** in separate'.
- Also try mispronouncing some of them in a way that will help you remember how to spell them, for example 'parl-**i-a**-ment', 'se-**par**-ate'.

Be prepared to feed back your best suggestions to the class. You will be tested on these words later in the lesson.

 Add up to five of these words to your spelling log if you've had difficulty in spelling them, and include your strategies for remembering them.

Introduction   as a class

Everyone has a wide range of registers that they use when speaking. You know just what tone of voice and language to use when you want to persuade a parent to buy you something, or what voice to use when you want to impress your friends. These are different registers, or levels of formality.

In addition, many people also speak in **dialect** when talking informally or **colloquially**. Their speech therefore contains many examples of non-Standard English.

The story that your teacher is about to read to you, 'The Celebrated Jumping Frog', is a good example of a story written both in dialect and in a colloquial register (**Worksheets 74a–b**).

> **colloquial** to do with conversation. Colloquial language is used in familiar, informal contexts.
> **dialect** a variety of English, often based on region, which has distinctive grammar and vocabulary

beautiful	fulfil	parallel	separate
business	height	parallelogram	skilful
conscience	knowledge	parliament	straight
consequence	listening	physical	technique
encyclopaedia	necessary	queue	weight

Its author, Mark Twain, has chosen not only to tell this story in the first person, but also to write in the dialect of an 'old timer' from the American wild west. When you listen to the story it is as if the old timer himself were speaking, telling you a story about another old timer called Jim Smiley.

While your teacher is reading you the story, think about how the storyteller's way of speaking adds to the interest of the story.

Development as a group

Both Mark Twain and Saki focused their stories on someone telling a story, but they have chosen very different types of English to do this in.

In groups, fill in the grid on **Worksheet 75** to analyse the different ways in which Mark Twain has made his story reflect the dialect of the speaker. Be prepared to feed back some of your examples.

Would it be possible to find examples of any of these features in Saki's story?

Plenary

What does Mark Twain's narrative approach add to the effectiveness of the story? How else could he have presented this story?

Be prepared to be tested on some of the words from the starter session.

homework

Add Mark Twain's 'The Celebrated Jumping Frog' to your reading record.

Next lesson you are going to be asked to tell a story about an incident – it could be autobiographical (something that has happened to you), biographical (something that has happened to someone else) or fictional (made up). Your homework is to think about what story you are going to tell and how you are going to tell it in the most entertaining manner. Decide how formal you want your language to be. Your story should last no longer than three minutes.

Telling a story

Aims

On these two pages you will:

- Think about how to tell a story in a way that engages your audience, recognizing the importance of pace, tone, mood and emphasis.
- Reflect on your development as a speaker and identify areas for improvement.
- Write a story that successfully conveys an incident through effective selection of words and sentence structure.

Starter
on your own

Your teacher is going to read you a short extract from the book *Kestrel for a Knave* by Barry Hines, which is set in a mining community in the 1960s (**Worksheet 76**). The central character, the misfit Billy, has to tell his class a story. Listen carefully and jot down all the ways in which this story engages the interest of his class. Think about how the storyteller's Barnsley dialect adds to the effectiveness of his story. Also think about how the speaker of such a story needs to deliver it in order to hold their audience's attention. You may want to highlight and annotate your copy of the story to indicate the following:

- Pace
- Tone
- Change of mood
- Emphasis
- How to make the ending effective.

Be prepared to feed back your ideas so that you can agree as a class on what to aim for when telling a story. Make a list of the best of your ideas, like the one opposite.

Introduction
as a group

Now it's your turn. In your groups, each of you in turn tells the story you've planned for homework. Consider all the points you thought about earlier, on how to make a spoken story engage the listener. Remember: no story should last longer than three minutes – it could be much shorter. Once you have heard all of your group's stories, decide which story was the most effective using the criteria the class has just agreed.

Be prepared to explain your choice to the class. You may decide that some stories sound so good, the whole class should hear them.

on your own

Reflect on how you could improve the presentation of your story, and note down two targets for improving your presentation when telling a story.

Ingredients for engaging your audience when storytelling

1. Introduce your story in a way that grabs your audience's attention

Listen to some of the openings of the stories and decide what makes them effective.

homework

Complete your story for homework.

> ! **Remember** to read your work through and redraft it if necessary so that you have achieved just the effect you want. Once it's complete, proofread your work. Then write a brief comment on how well you think you have completed the task.

Development on your own

Select any one of the stories you have heard today and write it as an effective short story. Decide on how you are going to narrate this story. Here are two possible choices:

- *Autobiographical style*, like Mark Twain, when you write in the **persona** of the narrator (this makes your writing very personal and probably informal)

- *Omniscient author*, like Saki, when you write as if you know about everything in the story (this can make your writing more distant and is liable to be more formal).

Now select the words and sentence structure that will create just the effect you want and which will help your readers picture the scene. Use your whiteboard or a piece of paper to help you draft the sort of sentences you want. Ensure your beginning will grab the reader's attention. You may want your characters to speak in colloquial English or in dialect.

persona a character taken on by someone

Your school library will have hundreds of wonderful short stories in it. You may wish to read more short stories by Mark Twain or Saki, or try Roald Dahl's *Tales of the Unexpected* ('Kiss Kiss' or 'Someone Like You'), Joan Aiken's 'Who Goes Down This Dark Road?' or Bill Naughton's 'Goalkeeper's Revenge'. There are collections of short stories on a whole range of different genres such as horror, mystery, sport and science fiction – just select the area that interests you.

Keep a note in your reading record of which stories you've read and mark with an asterisk those you would recommend to others.

Traditional tales

Aims

On these two pages you will:

- Consider why storytellers make particular choices, and analyse how patterns of language help structure text.
- Develop your understanding of prepositions.

Starter  as a group

Read the extract below. It is one of the tales of Nasreddin Hodja.

Look at all the prepositions highlighted in the story and decide how you would define the function of prepositions. Be prepared to feed back your ideas.

How Long Will It Take?

One day Nasreddin Hodja was chopping wood close **to** the road a few kilometres **from** Akshehir. **After** a while a man came **along** the road, walking **toward** Akshehir, and he called **to** the Hodja, 'Can you tell me how long it will take me **to** get **to** Akshehir?'

The Hodja heard him and looked **up from** his work, but he said nothing. So the man called again, louder this time, 'How long will it take me **to** get **to** Akshehir?'

Still the Hodja said nothing, and this time the man roared like a lion, 'How long will it take me **to** get **to** Akshehir?'

When the Hodja did not answer even then, the man decided he must be deaf, and so he started walking rapidly **toward** the city. Nasreddin Hodja watched him **for** a moment, and then he shouted, 'It will take you **about** an hour!'

'Well, why didn't you say so before?' demanded the man angrily.

'First I had **to** know how fast you were going **to** walk,' answered the Hodja.

Introduction in pairs

Listen carefully while your teacher reads two more tales of Nasreddin Hodja (**Worksheet 77**) and think about how you might answer the following questions. Your teacher will give you time to discuss your ideas with a partner.

1 Although the stories are very short, you learn quite a lot about the Hodja's character from them. What do you learn and how do you know this?

2 Is the listener or reader likely to be on the Hodja's side? Why?

3 What assumptions are made about the reader? (Look at the beginning of each of the stories: how do they differ from other stories you have read?)

4 Would a Turkish storyteller be able to assume their audience would know what a hafiz was?

5 Why do you think the storyteller uses so much repetition in 'How Long Will It Take?'?

The 500 or so tales of Nasreddin Hodja, a national institution in Turkey, have been translated into all the major languages in the world. The stories may date from as early as the 12th century. 'Hodja' is a term of respect for both a priest and a teacher. Nasreddin Hodja is normally pictured as a tubby figure in a turban riding a donkey. He is alternately stupid and shrewd, naive and wise, a noodlehead and a loveable conman.

6 What difference does it make that the Hodja doesn't always come out the winner?

7 What structural features do the three tales of Nasreddin Hodja that you have read have in common? What stylistic features do they have in common?

8 Now that you have read some of these stories, would you expect other tales of Nasreddin Hodja to end in a particular way?

Development

These versions of the tales of Nasreddin Hodja have been taken from a book called *Tales Alive in Turkey*, which is made up of recordings of everyday people retelling traditional stories. Such storytelling is referred to as the **oral tradition**. Because the stories were originally passed on by word of mouth, there are often many slightly different written versions of the same story. The notes at the back of the book provide a commentary on each story, informing the reader when and where each one was recorded plus other details. Listen carefully while your teacher reads you the commentary on 'How Long Will it Take?' (below).

as a group

In groups, discuss the following questions and be prepared to feed back your ideas:

1 What does this commentary add to your appreciation of the story?

2 What is the purpose of the preposition 'to' in the last sentence?

3 Why do you think that these stories have survived and been retold endlessly for at least the last 500 years?

> **oral tradition** the way in which traditional stories are handed down from one generation to the next by word of mouth; such stories are not written down until later

Narrator: Ahmet Kıygı
Site of recording: Ankara
Date collected: May 1962

Although this is a tale with fairly wide distribution in rural Turkey, the version we have included was collected in Ankara. It is one of the few in our archive not collected on tape, for it was told by the family doctor of the two editors in the course of an ordinary conversation. Asked when the seriously ill member of the family would be well enough to travel, Dr Kıygı responded that that would depend upon the patient's rate of recovery. Then, to illustrate the point, he told this Nasreddin Hodja story.

Plenary

In what key ways do these stories differ from stories like 'The Storyteller' or 'The Celebrated Jumping Frog'?

Add the tales of Nasreddin Hodja to your reading record.

Writing reviews

Aims

On these two pages you will:

- Analyse the structure and style of two book reviews.
- Write your own book review, identifying the book's potential readers and helping them to understand the book's context and its likely impact on them.
- Practise using noun phrases.
- Check your spelling with a dictionary and/or a spell-checker.

Starter

Listen carefully while your teacher reads you the following book review from the teenage book magazine *Boox*.

1 Reviews often give the reader insight into the **context** of the story and the role this plays in influencing events. From this brief review, what do you learn of the context in which *Nightjohn* is set?

2 You have two minutes to discuss with a partner the key structural and stylistic features of this short text. Consider especially the following points:

- Structure
- Tense
- Person.

Be prepared to feed your ideas back to the class.

Writing a brief review like this can be difficult. The tricky bit is making your plot **synopsis** short, snappy and interesting. Expanded noun phrases – highlighted in the *Nightjohn* example – come in handy here, as you can pack in a lot of information in an interesting way.

> **context** the background to a text, which may include the effect of the place and time in which the author lived
>
> **synopsis** summary

Nightjohn
by Gary Paulsen

Life is brutal for Sarny, **a slave girl on a plantation**, until she meets another slave, Nightjohn, **who believes that the ability to read and write is the key which will help unlock the chains of <u>oppression</u>[1] and <u>empower</u>[2] the slaves.** It broadened my mind about equal rights for women and racial discrimination. **A disturbing, powerful and meaningful read**.

– Shazma Zaman, 14

How noun phrases work

Think about how the noun phrase *He* has been expanded in the sentences below:

He waited.

The boy waited.

The anxious boy waited.

The anxious boy waited, *hoping to be selected to play for the team*.

The anxious boy, who was hoping to be selected to play for the team, waited.

Hoping to be selected to play for the team, the anxious boy waited.

Noun phrases can be a single word – a noun or a pronoun – which can be expanded into a larger phrase. As you can see from the examples, you can expand noun phrases in a whole variety of ways, adding words or clauses before or after the noun or pronoun at the centre of the phrase.

[1] *cruel treatment*
[2] *give power to*

Introduction
as a class

Your teacher will read you a slightly longer review of J. K. Rowling's *Harry Potter and the Prisoner of Azkaban* from the Amazon website (**Worksheet 78**). Think about the structure of the review and then discuss the following questions, supplying evidence to support your answers.

1 Does the review identify the book's potential readers?
2 Does it help them understand the book's context?
3 Does the review indicate what effect the book may have on its readers?
4 What is the focus of each paragraph? Why do you think the reviewer has chosen to structure the review in this way?
5 How has the reviewer made her sentences interesting?
6 What person is the review written in?
7 Would the review make sense to someone who hadn't read the book?

Development
on your own

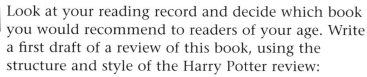

Look at your reading record and decide which book you would recommend to readers of your age. Write a first draft of a review of this book, using the structure and style of the Harry Potter review:

● **Paragraph 1:** An opening to hook the reader, followed by an introduction to the book's context covering the central theme with a few key details to intrigue the reader.

● **Paragraph 2:** Commentary on how the book develops, with a few unanswered questions to intrigue would-be readers. Conclude with a statement summing up the book's effect and who the target audience is.

Ensure that you have helped readers who have never read the book to understand the book's context and the impact it may have on them. Try to use expanded noun phrases effectively.

Your teacher will tell you how many minutes you have to complete a rough draft.

Plenary

Swap your draft with your partner's and read each other's draft carefully, bearing in mind the points that must be covered. In turn, discuss how each draft could be improved. Annotate your reviews with suggestions for improvement.

homework

Redraft your review for homework, making it as suitable as possible for its particular audience.

! **Remember** to check the structure of your review carefully. Proofread it and check that you have made no spelling or punctuation errors. Use a dictionary and/or a spell-checker and give the spelling a final check in context. Add to your spelling log the correct versions of any words you had difficulty with.
Finally write a brief comment stating why you think this final version is an improvement on your earlier draft.

Analysing the news on television

Aims

On these two pages you will:

- Make notes to analyse how news is presented on television.
- Analyse how television news is shaped by the technology of television and consider how this affects the nature of news.
- Develop listening skills, both when listening to news and to other people.
- Reflect on your strengths as a contributor to group discussion and set targets for your development.

Starter in pairs

Imagine that you were about to be interviewed in the street by a news team as a representative of today's youth. The question you are to be asked is 'Does pollution pose a danger to the planet?' You have two minutes to work out what you would say in answer. Your contribution will only be shown for a maximum of 30 seconds. Decide what points you would want to make in this very short **sound bite**.

> **sound bite** information that is packaged in a few words so that it fits nicely into very short interviews

Your teacher will now interview a few of you. But if you overrun your 30 seconds, be prepared to be interrupted by, 'Well, I'm afraid that's all we've got time for today, so it's back to the studio.'

What difference does it make when you've only got 30 seconds to explain your viewpoint?

Introduction as a group

The technology that is television – technology that is capable of bringing images, sounds and commentary on what is happening as it happens anywhere in the world – has changed our concept of what news is.

But rather than listening to your teacher telling you about how news is presented on TV or reading about it here, you're going to do some research yourselves. Your teacher will show you a ten-minute clip from a typical early evening news programme on ITV or BBC. Listen carefully while he or she explains how to fill in your section of the analysis grid on **Worksheet 79**. The news moves very fast so you'll need your wits about you to keep up. Your group will be focusing on one column, but you should also think about all the aspects so you can join in the class discussion later. You may need to watch the clip twice to check your findings.

Once you have completed your analysis discuss your findings with the rest of your group to see if you can agree. Try to ensure that you play a full part in this discussion, both as an active contributor and listener. Consider whether you altered or adapted your ideas in the light of what other people said.

Development *as a class*

Now discuss the following questions based on your analysis, and help your teacher fill in the analysis grid on **Worksheet 80**.

1 How many news items were covered in ten minutes?

2 What sort of items were selected? On average, how long was spent per item? How long was spent on the lead news item?

3 Why do you think this item was chosen as the lead item?

4 What length were the shortest and the longest interviews?

5 What use was made of technical effects, including visual images and sound effects? Why do you think these were included?

6 What was the role of the news presenter?

7 You only analysed the first ten minutes of the news. How do you think the presenter will close the programme?

8 What overall impression does the news programme want to give?

Once you have filled in the analysis grid, discuss the following questions. If you don't understand the points that others are making, be sure to ask questions to clarify or refine your understanding.

1 Why is a grid a useful device when you want to analyse something?

2 What difference have sound bites made to political debate?

3 Has the concept of 'news of the day' always existed?

4 Why is personal appearance now very important for politicians?

5 What difference do you think the presence of television cameras in Parliament has made to the debates there?

6 What difference do you think television has made to our concept of news?

Plenary

Reflect on your strengths and weaknesses when taking part in the group discussion and analysis. Use **Worksheet 81** to help you record your conclusions, and set two targets for how you could improve your contribution in discussions.

Minute	A. Timing Note length of each item and of any interviews within them	B. Topic of each item covered Note the key point/s of each	C. Selection Why did they include these items? What angle did they take? Consider what they left out	D. Role of main presenter Note how s/he fulfils the role – consider tone and expression; neutrality or bias	E. Technical effects including visual images and sound effects What are they and what purpose do they have?
1					
2					

Analysing front pages

Aims

On these two pages you will:

- Think about how changes in technology have contributed to the way news is presented in a newspaper.
- Analyse two newspaper articles, identifying how ideas can be developed in different ways.

Starter *as a group*

Today you're going to look at how two different newspapers use their front pages to present the same day's news. Look at the front pages of *The Mirror* (a tabloid newspaper) and *The Independent* (a broadsheet newspaper) from 2 May 2001.

See how many similarities or differences in layout you can identify. Your teacher will give you an analysis grid (**Worksheet 82**) to help you.

Now look at the layout of the front page of *The Times* from 50 years ago. Add notes about the layout of this paper's front page to your grid.

Be prepared to feed back your ideas to the rest of the class and see if you can help complete the statements below.

> The key differences between the front page of a broadsheet newspaper like 'The Independent' and a tabloid newspaper like 'The Mirror' are ...
>
> The key differences between the front page of a newspaper 50 years ago and that of today's newspapers are ...
>
> The appearance of newspapers has changed so greatly over the past 50 years because ...

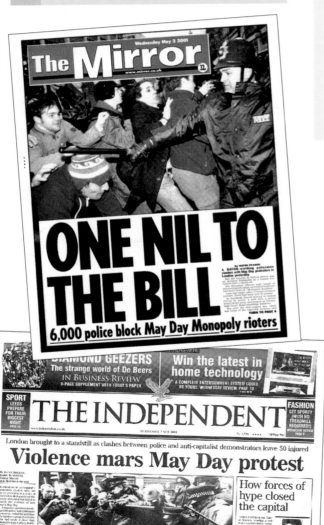

Introduction

Before looking more closely at the content of the **lead articles** of the two contemporary papers, look at the planning frame below. This is sometimes used to help train journalists to write newspaper articles, as the structure helps the writer to develop ideas clearly.

News article planning frame
- Introductory paragraph(s) with main news focus which hooks the reader's interest and answers basic questions like Who? What? Why? Where? and When?
- Paragraph(s) with less important news relating to main topic, including a quotation about how a character in the story feels.
- Paragraph(s) with least important news relating to main topic.
- Final paragraph to act as a pointer – either summing up the view or angle of the writer, or suggesting how the story may develop.

> **lead article** the main article on a newspaper or magazine page

Now follow carefully as your teacher reads you the lead article from *The Mirror* on 2 May 2001 and the opening five paragraphs from the lead article of *The Independent* of the same day (**Worksheet 83**).

In pairs, discuss whether both articles basically follow the structure outlined above. Be prepared to feed back your ideas.

Development in pairs

Now look at the way in which the opening paragraphs of the articles are written, focusing on the patterns of language used as well as what they're about. Be prepared to feed back your ideas and provide supporting evidence on the following questions. You may find it useful to annotate a copy of the articles.

1 Which is the easier to read?
2 Which is the more informal text?
3 What differences in tone are there?
4 Which uses more complex sentences and a wider vocabulary?
5 Which has the shorter paragraphs? Why?
6 Which uses more **emotive** language?
7 Which attempts to generalize about the significance of the event?
8 Which helps you to understand more fully what actually happened?

> **emotive** designed to create emotion in the audience

Plenary

What are the key visual differences between the front page of a tabloid newspaper and that of a broadsheet?

How is this related to developments in technology?

Evaluating a website

Aims

On these two pages you will:

- Look at how text and images on a website are influenced by the technological nature of websites.
- Consider whether the form of a website changes the meaning of the information it contains.
- Evaluate the structure and content of a website against agreed criteria.
- Explore the use of modal verbs like can/could, may/might, must/ought.
- Look at how connectives like 'if', 'however', 'unless' and 'although' help you to express reservation.

Starter  in pairs

In pairs, quickly list all the advantages a good news website could have over news in a newspaper or on TV. Be prepared to share your ideas with the rest of the class so that the class can establish a list of criteria for good news websites.

Your teacher will display the class's agreed final list, as you will need it later.

- Do all the points on the list depend on the technological nature of websites?
- What sort of text is most suited to websites?

Once the list has been established, your teacher will model for you what happens if you rephrase your criteria so that each point begins with the following words:

If you were looking at news on a website rather than in a newspaper, you …

For example:

If you were looking at news on a website rather than in a newspaper, you would be able to join in the debate through email or discussion boards.

 on your own

Use your whiteboard or a piece of paper to see if you can express another one of your criteria in this way.

As you can see, you've used phrases like '**would** be able' or '**could**' – just as, when you're evaluating anything, you often use phrases like:

- It **would** have been better if …
- It **might** have been better if …
- If I **could** do this again, I would …
- It **ought** to have included …

The words highlighted are all **modal verbs**. Modal verbs are important when you are evaluating anything because they allow you to move from what *is* to what *could be*.

Connectives such as 'if' help you express reservation. Other useful connectives when evaluating and expressing reservations are: 'although', 'unless', 'however', 'except', 'yet' and 'apart from'.

modal verb a type of auxiliary (or 'helper') verb which expresses possibility (can, might), speculation (could, might), permission (can, may), obligation (ought, should) or necessity (should, must)

Introduction `in pairs`

In pairs, look at the news section of the BBC's website (http://news.bbc.co.uk/) and use the criteria you established in the starter session to evaluate this website. Fill in the grid on **Worksheet 84** to help you. You can add your own criteria if you have points you want to make that the class criteria did not cover.

Development `on your own`

Write up your findings, using the structure of your evaluation grid to help you. Make sure that you have used modal verbs and connectives that express reservation. Below are some sentence starters that may be useful.

- *The design of the home page was …*
- *Having an image accompanied by a sound bite made it …*
- *Being able to click for additional information made it …*
- *It could have been improved by …*
- *It would have been better if …*
- *If there had been …*
- *However, a less impressive feature was …*
- *Although the front page was …*

All the above sentence starters are in the third person. You may wish to include personal opinion in the final paragraph of your evaluation, in which case you could use a first-person sentence starter such as these:

- *I particularly liked the way …*
- *The pages I liked best were …*

Plenary

Listen to some of the opening paragraphs of the evaluations and see if you agree with the points being made. Do any of them contain modal verbs or connectives that express reservation?

Complete the following statement on your whiteboard or a piece of paper: *Websites could affect the meaning of information because …*

homework

Complete your evaluation for homework. Make certain that you've used modal verbs effectively.

> **!** **Remember** to read through your work carefully, improve it if necessary and write a brief comment saying how well you think you have completed the task.
> **Warning:** Do not write 'would of', 'should of' or 'could of' – this is always grammatically incorrect. Write 'would have', 'could have', 'should have', or (when writing in less formal contexts) abbreviate this to 'would've', 'could've', 'should've'.

Writing a balanced analysis

Aims

On these two pages you will:

- Develop your note-taking skills, using grids to analyse and compare different texts.
- Present a balanced analysis of the way three different newspapers treat a news story, supporting your analysis with evidence from the texts.
- Trace the development of values and ideas in three editorials.

Starter *as a group*

Look at the front pages of three tabloid national newspapers from 9 January 2001 (**Worksheet 85**), the day the news broke that the killers of James Bulger had been granted the right to a life of anonymity (that is, they could change their names and identity). In your group:

1 Look at these front pages and analyse the way the different papers chose to allocate space to this particular item.

2 Think about what values the headlines convey.

3 Fill in the top two rows of the analysis grid (**Worksheet 86**). Can you think why *The Mirror* may have chosen not to feature this news on its front page, unlike every other national paper that day?

Introduction *as a class*

Your teacher will now read you the editorial comment on this story from the *Daily Mail* (**Worksheet 87**). Listen carefully and join in discussion of the following questions. As you listen to the discussion, fill in the relevant sections on the analysis grid (**Worksheet 86**).

- What is the *Daily Mail*'s key reason for thinking the decision was very wrong?
- How does the *Daily Mail* support and develop its argument that this is a dangerous precedent (that is, a legal decision that sets a pattern for future judgements in similar cases)?
- What words or phrases are highly emotive?
- What does the *Daily Mail* have to say about press freedom?
- How does the *Daily Mail* support and develop this argument?

as a group

Now look at the editorials on the same day from *The Sun* and *The Mirror* (**Worksheet 88**). Decide whether they support or oppose the judge's decision and identify the key arguments that they use to support their position. Jot the key points down on the analysis grid in the appropriate columns. Make sure you keep the grid carefully as you will need it in the next lesson.

Be prepared to feed back your conclusions to the class.

THE SUN SAYS

Justice kept in the dark

One of our greatest judges, Lord Denning, said justice must not only be done, it must be seen to be done.

Development *on your own*

Your task is to write the following essay:

Present a **balanced** analysis, with supporting evidence, of how three newspapers treated the judgement that the Bulger killers should be granted a life of anonymity.

balanced not taking sides; a balanced analysis presents information factually without trying to bias the reader towards any viewpoint

Watch carefully while your teacher models how you might introduce your essay:

On Tuesday 9 January 2001 'The Daily Mail', 'The Sun' and 'The Daily Mirror' all chose to focus their editorials on the judgement that granted James Bulger's killers a life of anonymity. However, each newspaper took a different approach ...

Now try writing this essay yourself, using your analysis grid. The following structure may help you:

- Compare and contrast the papers' front-page treatment of this news.
- Compare and contrast the overall editorial approaches to this issue (quote the headlines as evidence).
- Focus on a few key issues from the editorials and how these were developed, bringing out any similarities or differences (select brief quotes from the editorials to support your points).

- Conclusion: sum up the overall differences and draw attention to the complexity of the issue.

Useful connectives

To indicate contrasting viewpoints:
- On the other hand,
- Whereas,
- In contrast,
- From a different perspective,

To introduce evidence:
- For example,
- As illustrated by,
- As shown by,

To indicate closure:
- In conclusion,

Plenary

Discuss the ingredients that you have to include to achieve a balanced analysis of an issue.

homework

Complete your essay for homework.

> **!** *Remember* to read your work through carefully, ensuring that you have achieved a balanced approach, supported by evidence. Improve your essay if necessary and write a brief comment saying how well you have completed the task.

VOICE OF The Mirror   voice@mirror.co.uk

A lifetime in the shadows
The killing of James Bulger was one of the most terrible crimes of modern times.

Presenting a commentary

Aims

On these two pages you will:

- Decide on the best structure to help you plan and draft a presentation on how three newspapers treated a news story.
- Present your commentary, supporting it with visual aids.
- Develop your vocabulary and spelling by recognizing how words may be linked by root.
- Develop your spelling by recognizing similar ways of spelling specific sounds.

Starter  as a group

Some of the words listed below can be grouped together by shared roots, such as 'view' and 'viewpoint', which gives them some meaning in common. Others can be grouped together by spelling pattern, for example 'rough' and 'tough'.

Your teacher will give you all these words on cards (**Worksheet 89**). See if you can sort the words into two groups:

- Words that are related by root (and thus by meaning)
- Words that are related by spelling.

Can you work out what all the words related by root mean?

Introduction on your own

You started this unit by considering how the news is presented on television, including the role of the presenter. Today, it's your turn to be the presenter. You're going to turn the written commentary you've just completed – on the way three newspapers treated the judgement that the killers of James Bulger should be granted anonymity – into a spoken commentary supported by visual aids.

Remember, to be effective your talk must engage your listeners. You must not read your commentary; instead, draw up a list of the key points you want to make so that they can act as a prompt when you speak. Use your whiteboard or a piece of paper to help you. Your teacher will model for you how to do this.

Look at the analysis grid you completed in the last lesson (**Worksheet 86**). This is a summary of the key points you can select from when making your presentation.

editorial	viewpoint	interview	geography
view	quite	enough	editor
edge	edit	write	light
graph	telegraph	graphics	interviewer
television	judge	telephone	rough
badge	graphical	fright	slight
tough	edition	grudge	interviewee
bright	sight	polite	

There are basically two different ways you can structure your presentation:

- **Structure A: Paper by paper.** Present each paper in turn, referring back to those looked at earlier as appropriate. If you choose this structure, select the key points you wish to make for each paper – highlight these in the relevant columns on your grid, using a different colour for each paper.

- **Structure B: Aspect by aspect.** Take each aspect in turn and draw out the differences. If you choose this approach, select the aspects you wish to focus on – highlight these in the relevant rows on your grid, using a different colour for each aspect selected.

(Note: structure A is easier to control; structure B is potentially more interesting but can lead to audience confusion.)

Now follow these steps:

1 Decide which approach you want to take.

2 Select the key points that you want to make.
You do not have to cover everything. It would be better to select a few key points and make these clearly. It may be useful to use a blank copy of the news analysis grid (**Worksheet 86**) to jot down the points you've decided to focus on.

3 Practise talking through your points and decide if you want to amend your plan.
The best way to help yourself is to see if you can briefly run through all the points you want to make in the right order. (Remember what you noted about the role of news presenters when you did your analysis of TV news on page 95.)

4 Work out what visual aids you want to use to support your presentation.
Make sure you arrange any visual aids you are going to use in the right order so that they are to hand when you need them.

Development *as a group*

Your teacher will set a time limit on your preparations, after which you will each in turn present your commentary to your group. Your teacher will be coming round and seeing which presentations are working well. You should feed back advice on how to improve each other's presentations.

Reflect on what targets you need to set yourself to improve your speaking skills and include them in the review of what you've learnt (page 104).

Plenary

Watch and listen carefully while two or three presentations are given to the whole class. Join in the class discussion on what elements made these presentations successful.

Reviewing what's been learnt

In this section you have increased your understanding and practice of the skills of writing, especially short story writing.

- You have focused on how writers select particular words or sentence structures to convey particular meanings, and how they make endings effective.
- You've also considered the needs of specific audiences and written a review with this in mind.
- As a reader, you have questioned meanings, motives and assumptions.

You have also analysed how news is defined and presented in different media. In particular you have:

- Analysed a news website and a TV news programme.
- Written up how different newspapers present the same news event.
- Considered how the medium itself affects what is presented.
- Looked at the role of presenters and tried being a presenter yourself.

You should have extended your vocabulary and improved your spelling, as well as increased your understanding of how the English language works.

Now it's time to think about what things you have learnt from this section, and list the key points in your exercise book, using these sentence starters to help you:

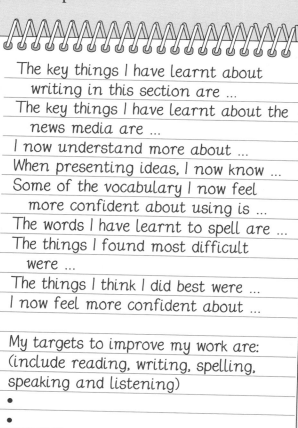

The key things I have learnt about writing in this section are ...
The key things I have learnt about the news media are ...
I now understand more about ...
When presenting ideas, I now know ...
Some of the vocabulary I now feel more confident about using is ...
The words I have learnt to spell are ...
The things I found most difficult were ...
The things I think I did best were ...
I now feel more confident about ...

My targets to improve my work are: (include reading, writing, spelling, speaking and listening)
-
-
-
-

Plan, draft, present

Introduction

In this section you will look at extracts written by recent and contemporary playwrights. Two of these were written by established scriptwriters, and the third was developed by drama teachers in a school with the help of students like yourselves.

At first you're going to focus on the skills these writers have used to craft their scripts. Then you're going to improvise your own scene and develop this into a scripted scene which you will present.

Later you're going to take on the role of a member of a group presenting a bid at a council meeting. After this you will develop your writing skills by planning and drafting a formal report of the meeting, before evaluating both your work and that of others.

Key aims

In this section you will:

- Develop your skills in understanding and interpreting dramatic roles and presenting ideas.
- Develop your skills in writing a formal report.

Interpreting a scene (1)

Aims

On these two pages you will:

- Read an extract from a play, analyse its structure and, through revising your interpretation, decide how to present it.
- Explore and develop relationships through acting the role of a seven-year-old convincingly and reflect on your performance, keeping an evaluative record of your contribution.
- Further develop your understanding of the difference between Standard English and dialect.

Starter *as a group*

Your teacher is going to read you the stage directions from the beginning of scene 5 of Dennis Potter's play *Blue Remembered Hills*. The play is set in the West Country on a summer afternoon during the Second World War. The childish games, fantasies and bullying of seven children end in tragedy. In scene 5 three of the seven-year-old children are imitating adults by 'playing house'.

The children's speech reflects their Forest of Dean dialect as well as their fantasies. In the Analyse section (pages 86–87) you did some work on dialect and colloquial speech which you are going to develop today. Your first task, in groups of three, is to read the extract from scene 5 (**Worksheets 90a–b**) and amend the highlighted words on the first page so that the children are saying the same things but in Standard English, as in the example (right).

This will be easier if each of you takes on one role and focuses on adapting your part. You will also then be in a better position to understand how to **interpret** the play and your role. Be prepared to present some of your version to the class.

Introduction *as a group*

In your groups, discuss your initial impressions of the scene. How did this influence the way you read it?

Each group will probably have read the scene in a slightly different way because they will have interpreted it differently. Sometimes, when you hear someone else's interpretation, you want to revise your ideas.

as a class

Discuss the following questions about the techniques Potter has used to make the scene effective and listen carefully to people's ideas – you may wish to adapt your interpretation of your part as a result of these ideas.

AUDREY What ~~dost thee~~ *do you* know about it, Donald Duck? You ~~ant~~ *have* never had a ~~babby~~ *baby*.

DONALD ~~I be~~ *I am* supposed to be the daddy here, ~~byunt I~~ *am I not*? And – and – don't call me Donald Duck.

---

interpret to present a piece of writing or music so that a particular meaning is given to it

1 Why does the scene begin with detailed stage directions about the children, particularly Donald?

2 Why did the playwright make the children speak in dialect?

3 Why did he make Audrey so spiteful in the opening of the scene?

4 Why doesn't Audrey want to play the role of Angela's daughter?

5 Where do the children get their ideas about how married couples speak to and treat each other?

6 Why does Angela suddenly turn on Donald as well?

7 What difference does this make to the development of the scene?

8 What does the scene tell you about Donald's life at home?

9 How has the playwright structured this scene to build up tension?

10 Why has the playwright made the children mix their pretend roles and their real selves? How is this effective?

Development as a group

Discuss how your group is going to present the scene in light of the class discussion. Then rehearse the scene, bringing out your group's interpretation.

Think about how you will emphasize:
- Audrey's spitefulness
- Donald's desire to be seen as the man of the house
- The fact that these are seven-year-olds playing at being adults
- The build up of tension at the end of the scene.

Watch carefully as some groups present their interpretation of the scene, and decide what makes one presentation more effective than another.

Plenary

Discuss which of the interpretations worked best and why. Reflect on how you could have improved your own contribution.

Your teacher will explain to you how you are going to record your contribution to dramatic improvisation and presentation in this section of work. Complete your drama record (**Worksheet 91**), evaluating your contribution and considering how it could have been improved. Here is an example of the sort of entry you could make:

Date	Role/activity	Focus	Evaluation	Targets for improvement
12 June 2002	Interpretation of Audrey from Dennis Potter's **Blue Remembered Hills**	Bring out spitefulness of character	Delivered lines in convincing manner but only in role when speaking – also didn't bring out the differences between Audrey as Audrey and Audrey as nurse	• React in character to what other characters are saying • Bring out all aspects of character

Interpreting a scene (2)

Aims

On these two pages you will:

- Develop your skills as critical readers, discussing the structure, techniques and style of a scene from a radio play.
- Interpret the scene, and revise your interpretation in the light of discussion.
- Explore and develop relationships through your work in role and keep an evaluative record of your contribution.
- Explore spelling patterns and recognize exceptions to these patterns.

Starter *in pairs*

1   Read the poem 'English' (right) and see if you can agree on how it should be read out loud without making any pronunciation mistakes. Focus on the verse you have been allocated by your teacher, but read the whole poem so that you understand the context. Be prepared to read your verse aloud to the class.

2   Look at all the highlighted words in the version on **Worksheet 92**. Focusing on your verse, underline any of these words that you both agree conform to a regular spelling pattern. Can you think of three other words that conform to the same spelling pattern? Jot these down on your whiteboards.

3   Do you know what all the highlighted words on the worksheet version mean?

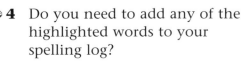

4   Do you need to add any of the highlighted words to your spelling log?

English

I take it you already know
Of tough and bough and cough and dough?
Others may stumble, but not you
On hiccough, thorough, slough and through?
Well done! And now you wish, perhaps
To learn of less familiar traps?

Beware of heard, a dreadful word
That looks like beard and sounds like bird.
And DEAD; it is said like bed, not bead;
For goodness sake, don't call it deed!
Watch out for meat and great and threat
(They rhyme with suite and straight
    and debt).
A moth is not a moth in mother,
Nor both in bother, broth in brother.

And here is not a match for there,
Nor dear and fear for bear and pear,
And then there's dose and rose and lose –
Just look them up – and goose and choose,
And cork and work and card and ward
And font and front and word and sword.
And do and go, then thwart and cart,
Come, come, I have hardly made a start.

A dreadful language? Why, man alive,
I'd learned to talk it when I was five,
And yet to write it, the more I tried,
I hadn't learned it at fifty-five.

Richard N. Krogh

Introduction as a class

The radio play *Unman, Wittering and Zigo* by Giles Cooper was first broadcast in 1958, and adapted by the author for television in 1965. It is set in a private boarding school for boys when a new teacher, Mr John Ebony, takes up his first teaching post mid-year with a senior class. He has been informed by the headteacher that the class's previous teacher, Mr Pelham, had an unfortunate accident – he fell over the local cliff in a fog and died. Mr Ebony's class are not slow to tell him that, far from being an accident, they killed Mr Pelham. The headteacher refuses to listen and so Mr Ebony is left with the task not only of trying to control the class but also of working out who exactly is responsible for Mr Pelham's death.

Scene 3 (**Worksheets 93a–b**) shows what happens when Mr Ebony first meets his new class. Read the scene together and think about how it is presented. Discuss your initial impressions of the scene.

Now discuss the following questions:

1 Why do you think the writer decided to open this scene with the class register?

2 How can you tell that the teacher doesn't know the class?

3 What is the most noticeable thing about the class's behaviour?

4 Which lines best illustrate how tricky the class is to deal with?

5 Every now and again, the whole class speaks as one (indicated by *omnes*, the Latin word for 'all'). Why do you think Giles Cooper included this feature?

6 What sort of register (colloquial/formal etc) do the class speak in?

7 Who is the class victim? Does Mr Ebony deal effectively with this?

8 How is the scene structured to help the audience understand how difficult the class is to control?

9 Do you think Mr Ebony is going to control the class or the class control Mr Ebony? What evidence do you have to support your view?

10 What does this scene suggest about how people sometimes treat each other?

Think about how the scene was initially presented in the class reading. Would you interpret it differently in the light of the discussion you've just had?

Development as a group

Your teacher will divide you into groups of eight to ten and allocate everyone a role. Discuss and rehearse how you are going to interpret the scene, bringing out the tensions of the scene and highlighting how people treat each other. Each group in turn will then present their interpretation to the class.

Plenary

Discuss which interpretation was the most effective and reflect on how you could have improved your own interpretation.

homework

Fill in your drama record (**Worksheet 91**) for homework, evaluating your contribution and considering what you would improve next time.

Interpreting a scene (3)

Aims

On these two pages you will:

- Develop your skills as critical readers, discussing the structure, techniques and style of a play extract.
- Interpret the role of a family member as the family faces breakdown, and explore and develop relationships through your work in role.

- Keep an evaluative record of your contribution to the presentation and evaluate the presentation of others.
- Think about how changing the tense affects a text.

Starter *as a class*

The scene you are about to study today from *You Made Me* begins like this. (The tense of the verbs is indicated in the margin.)

COLLINS PLAYS PLUS
You Made Me
Kelvin Reynolds and Adrian Lockwood

Scene Three: Counselling

present — *Waiting room.* **Kelly, Lucy, Alan**
present — *and the* **Silent Child** *(who <u>sits</u> alone away from the others).* **Lucy**
present — *<u>plays</u> with a board game.* **Kelly**
present — *<u>reads</u> a magazine. Characters*
present — *<u>freeze</u>.*

KELLY *(to audience)* I suppose it
past — <u>was</u> like that for me. My own
past — private war, <u>played</u> out inside
past — my head as I <u>took</u> refuge under
past — the covers. I <u>couldn't</u> always
past — hear what they <u>were</u> arguing
about, trivial things really, but
present — it <u>doesn't</u> really matter. What
past — <u>did</u> they get so angry about?
past — I'd <u>lie</u> awake for ages
past — wondering if they <u>knew</u> I <u>could</u>
past — <u>hear</u> them, until it <u>passed</u>. And
past — it always <u>did</u>.

Discuss with the person sitting next to you the reason for these changes of tense. Be prepared to share your ideas with the class.

The playwrights have chosen to make Kelly tell her memories of her parents' break up in the past tense. They could have chosen to have her tell them in the present tense. Listen carefully while your teacher reads you the revised version.

KELLY *(to audience)* I suppose it <u>is</u> like this for me. My own private war, <u>playing</u> out inside my head as I <u>take</u> refuge under the covers. I <u>can't</u> always hear what they <u>are</u> arguing about, trivial things really, but it <u>doesn't</u> really matter. What <u>do</u> they get so angry about? I <u>lie</u> awake for ages wondering if they <u>know</u> I <u>can</u> <u>hear</u> them, until it <u>passes</u>. And it always <u>does</u>.

Discuss with the person sitting next to you what difference this change of tense makes. Be prepared to share your ideas with the class.

Introduction as a group

Today you're going to analyse and present a scene from *You Made Me* by Kelvin Reynolds and Adrian Lockwood in preparation for developing your own scene about a family row. *You Made Me* is a play about how the break up of relationships between parents can damage their children.

In scene 3 (**Worksheets 94a–b**) the children of four different broken relationships meet up in the waiting room of a family counselling centre. The children are:

- Two sisters, Kelly and Lucy
- A brother and sister, Wayne and Leanne
- An only child, Alan
- A silent nameless child.

In groups of six, decide who will play each role; the silent child should also be the director of the scene. Read the scene as a group and discuss the following questions:

1 Why does the scene begin with a **freeze frame**?

2 What difference does it make that Kelly's opening **monologue** is directed to the audience?

3 How are you going to present the opening of the scene to make it effective?

4 What do you know about the relationship between Kelly and Lucy from their opening conversation?

5 What sort of impression do Wayne and Leanne want to make? Which lines best express this?

6 Do all the characters use the same register?

7 What do you learn about Alan from this scene?

8 Why is the silent child silent?

9 How would you present the growing aggression at the end of this scene?

Decide how you will present the scene as a result of your discussion.

freeze frame an important moment in a play captured like a photograph to underline its significance

monologue a speech made directly to the audience which reveals a character's inner thoughts

Development as a group

Present your group's interpretation to the rest of the class. Points to remember:

- Make the opening freeze frame effective.
- Make Kelly address the audience directly with her opening monologue.
- Bring out the differences in character and how the children interact.
- Build up the tension towards the end of the scene.

Use the grid on **Worksheet 95** to evaluate each group's work.

Plenary

Discuss which presentation was the most effective and why. Reflect on how you could have improved your performance.

homework

Complete your drama record (**Worksheet 91**) for homework, evaluating your contribution and considering what you would improve in the light of the class discussion.

Improvising a scene

Aims

On these two pages you will:

- Improvise a scene about the break up of a family, exploring character and using dramatic techniques to engage the audience.
- Evaluate the improvisations.
- Revise your improvisation after discussion, then write a script for the scene, planning and drafting as appropriate.

Scenario

A family is on the verge of breaking up. The parents constantly pick on each other. The children play one parent against the other and squabble between themselves, sometimes smothering the baby with attention, at other times ignoring it. The grandmother has always been against the mother.

Characters

- father
- mother
- 2 children (2 girls or 2 boys or a girl and a boy)
- a baby
- grandmother (father's mother)

(Remember to name the characters)

Starter as a group

Look at the outline of a scene (above). In your group of six, decide who is going to take on each role. The baby should also be the director and chair the script writing. Remember that the more you can co-operate as a group, the greater chance there is of your improvisation being effective.

You have ten minutes to work out your improvisation. Use the planning frame on **Worksheet 96** to help you. You should consider the following points:

- What incident(s) your scene will focus on
- What aspects of the characters you will develop
- Whether the characters are going to be similar or contrasting
- The sort of dialogue that will reveal this
- How to set the scene to grab the audience's attention
- How to build up tension and vary pace
- What dramatic techniques to include
- How the end of the scene will make a lasting impression.

Introduction _as a class_

Present your improvisation and watch the improvisations of other groups. Use **Worksheet 97** to help you evaluate them. Discuss as a class which improvisations worked best and why.

Development _as a group_

Your task now is to make your improvisation the basis of a script for the scene. Follow these steps:

First discuss whether your improvisation worked or whether it needs significant alteration. Decide what key alterations need to be made. You may want to adapt the plan you made for your improvisation or make a new plan.

Now you are in a position to begin drafting your group script. Each member of the group should focus on developing their allotted character within the shape of the scene as a whole.

Once you have completed your first draft, begin to refine your script. Read it aloud and see if you think it works. Annotate your copy of the script with notes about how it could be improved. Consider action, reaction and facial expression, as well as what and how things are to be said. Remember that silence can be as significant as speech. Amend your script accordingly.

Using the annotated script to guide you, redraft your script.

Plenary

Each group should select up to three aspects of their script writing that have worked well and up to three that have caused problems. Be prepared to present your ideas to the class and see if the class can agree on a list of advice – 'The dos and don'ts of group script writing'.

homework

Familiarize yourself with your part in the script, and decide how you will deliver your lines and how you will react to the lines and actions of the other characters.

Presenting your scene

Aims

On these two pages you will:
- Explore how the tone of a sentence affects its meaning.
- Finalize your script, bearing in mind its effect on the audience.
- Present the scene, using a variety of dramatic techniques.
- Evaluate both your contribution to the presentation and the presentation of others.

Derek Bentley

Starter

In 1953 19-year-old Derek Bentley was hanged for the murder committed by his 16-year-old friend Christopher Craig, who was too young to be sentenced to death. Both young men were hiding on a roof from the police after a bungled burglary. Bentley is alleged to have said the words, 'Let him have it, Chris!'

He claimed that he had said this to try to persuade his friend to hand over his gun to the police. A police witness claimed Bentley had said it as if encouraging Craig to shoot the policeman.

In pairs, try saying the following sentences in different ways.

1 **'Let him have it, Chris!'** Try saying this:
   a) to persuade Chris to hand over the gun
   b) to encourage Chris to shoot the policeman.

2 **'What is wrong with you?'** Try saying this:
   a) to express genuine concern
   b) to suggest the person is a nuisance and is always pretending to be ill.

3 **'How very kind!'** Try saying this:
   a) to emphasize the person's kindness
   b) to suggest the opposite of what the words mean on the surface.

Your teacher will then ask for volunteers to illustrate these differences of tone. Remember that tone is central to meaning. The list below covers only a small number of the vast range of tones in which you can speak. Can you add to the list?

enthusiasm sarcasm aggression
pleading desperation boredom
rudeness

Introduction as a group

Complete the redrafting of your script (see page 113). Bear in mind what its effect will be on the audience. Then rehearse your scene. Remember to:

- Grab the audience's attention with the opening
- Bring out the cause/s of tension between the characters
- Vary pace and build up tension
- Make effective use of expression, tone and gesture
- Decide on the best use of space
- Make the ending memorable.

Development as a class

Perform your script to the class. Evaluate the performances of the other groups using **Worksheet 98**.

Plenary

Discuss which performance was the most effective and why. Fill in your drama record (**Worksheet 91**), reflecting on the role you played in the improvisation and in the scripted performance, and set targets for improving your performance.

Aims

On these two pages you will:

- Begin planning a group presentation in formal English.
- Recognize how formal contexts require particular word choices.
- Understand the precise meaning of specialist terms and check that you can spell them.

Starter *as a group*

For the rest of this section you're going to be focusing on preparing a presentation at a meeting and then writing a formal report. This will require selecting the formal language appropriate to the task.

Before you start on your presentation, you're going to review some specialist terms from across the curriculum.

brief	exhibit	solution
co-ordinate	expression	subject
cycle	illustrate	tense
demonstrate	production	trace
divide	scale	volume

These 15 words all have everyday meanings as well as specific subject meanings. Your group will be given five of these words plus cards that provide three things for you to match up (**Worksheets 99a–b**):

- the specific subject meaning of each word
- the everyday meaning of the word
- a sentence using the word in its everyday context.

For example:

current

Everyday definition
Something that is happening, being done or being used now

Everyday sentence
He is the current holder of the world record for the high jump.

Science definition
A flow of electricity through a wire or circuit

Now see if you can work out sentences that use each of the five words in their subject-specific context, so that the rest of the class understands what the words mean. For example:

Science sentence: An electric current is passed through the liquid.

Be prepared to present your sentences to the rest of the class. Finally, check that you can spell all 15 words. Focus on any of these words that you think you may have problems spelling, as your teacher will test you at the end of the lesson.

Scenario: The future of the Northfields site

The merger of two local schools has resulted in a <u>prime development site</u>[1] (<u>formerly</u>[2] Northfields School) becoming available in the centre of Bridgechester, a large <u>prosperous</u>[3] town which has retained excellent quality high street shops. The council initially proposed demolishing the school buildings and developing the

1 *top-quality site to build on*
2 *once*
3 *wealthy*
4 *public*

Introduction as a class

Read the scenario below. At this council meeting you will have two roles:

- A member of a development group making a presentation
- A local councillor evaluating the presentations.

1 Listen carefully while your teacher reads you the article from the *Bridgechester Echo* on **Worksheet 100**.

2 Consider how much local support each bid can depend on, quoting evidence from the article.

3 Is the newspaper article written in formal or informal language? What evidence do you have to support your opinion?

site into a municipal[4] car park. However, the site has attracted interest from a range of large developers. A special council meeting has been called to consider which of the five following bids should be granted planning permission:

- Car park proposal
- Spendulike supermarket
- Keep U Fit sports centre
- Community centre
- Flix R Us multiplex cinema development.

Development as a group

Your teacher will give you information about your group's bid (**Worksheet 101**). Discuss this in your group. Remember:

- You will have five minutes to present your case.
- Every member of the group must contribute to this presentation.
- This is a formal occasion, so Standard English will be appropriate – avoid colloquial language and expression.

Now begin planning the key arguments that you should make to support your bid. Use the planning frame on **Worksheet 102** to help you.

- Think about how your development could be presented as being in the town's best interests.
- Consider the possible arguments against your bid and decide how these could be countered.
- You may want to decide that a member of your group is a local resident who is speaking on behalf of your bid. Decide what sort of arguments they might use.

Once you've thought of all the arguments you can, use the grid on **Worksheet 103** to work out what specific points are going to be made by each member of the group and how the presentation is going to be structured.

Plenary

What do you think are the most important points to bear in mind when planning a presentation?

 Be prepared to be tested on some of the words you focused on at the beginning of the lesson. Add any words that you misspell to your spelling log, and remember to record any key terms from across the curriculum that you have difficulty in spelling. Try to add strategies for remembering them.

Polishing your presentation

Aims

On these two pages you will:

- Refine your formal presentation, considering appropriate rhetorical devices and the level of formality of the language.
- Discuss how the group could improve their presentation, seeking agreement and reporting the key suggestions.
- Reflect on your own contribution to the group presentation and identify points for improvement.
- Consider the vocabulary, sentence grammar and stylistic conventions of the writing you've been doing in all areas of the curriculum.

Starter **as a group**

Today you're going to start by reviewing the types of writing you have been doing in all your subjects this year. Your teacher will divide you into six groups. Each group will be given a different piece of Year 8 writing to analyse (**Worksheets 104a–b**). Your task is to discuss the text and see if you can agree the following:

- Text type: Is it Explanation, Information, Recount etc or a mixture of text types?
- Structure: Is it chronological or how is it structured?
- Stylistic conventions: Is it formal or informal; personal or impersonal?
- Sentence grammar: What sort of sentences are used – short and simple, complex or a mixture? What tense is it in?
- Vocabulary: Are there any examples of subject-specific vocabulary in it?

Annotate and highlight your text like the example below. Everyone should be prepared to contribute to presenting the conclusions of their group to the class.

Text type
Discursive – formal essay

Vocabulary
Specialist vocabulary related to literature

Style
Formal impersonal beginning – becomes more personal with use of first person plural. Formal language but uses colloquial term to describe Adrian, in keeping with style of book

Structure
Introductory paragraph. Good use of connectives to link ideas

The Secret Diary of Adrian Mole

The Secret Diary of Adrian Mole uses **cyclical narrative** where the story at the end returns to exactly where it started, with Adrian making his New Year's resolutions. This technique makes us believe that Adrian has made no development in growing up. But, as **we** look through the book, we can see that Adrian has actually developed from a **goofy** little kid into a normal mature adult.

Sentence grammar
The writer uses complex sentences. Mixture of present and past tense

Introduction (as a group)

Every member of the group should check that they are clear about the points that they are making in presenting their report (see page 117). Write a few words on a prompt card to help you remember what you want to say and in what order:

Local resident supporting Keep U Fit bid

Just what Bridgechester needs:

- Local interest in facilities
- Nearest gym over 50 km away
- Something for all ages
- Increase value of housing – bring trade.

Rehearse your presentation. Remember:

- Ensure everyone takes part
- Present your case in appropriate English – formal but personal
- Use a range of rhetorical devices:
  - repetition for effect
  - use of emotive, persuasive language
  - use of inclusive 'We'
  - direct appeal to audience
  - praise for town
  - change of tone
  - end on a high note.

Listen carefully to everyone's contribution and note down ways in which the presentation could be improved. Points to consider:

- Does the introduction clearly put the audience in the picture?
- Is the order of the presentation logical?
- Is each person helping to illustrate the key points?
- Does the presentation end effectively?

Development (as a group)

Using your notes to help you, evaluate the group's presentation as well as your own contribution. Try to agree what you need to change to make the presentation more effective. Decide on the final approach and amend your prompt card accordingly. Now rehearse your presentation for the final time.

Plenary

Feed back any key changes that your group decided to make to the group's presentation.

homework

Practise your presentation for homework. Reflect on your contribution to the presentation and set two or three targets to try to fulfil at the actual presentation next lesson.

! Remember

- Treat your presentation as if you were telling a story.
- Work out what you want to say in a manner and order that flows.
- Make certain the order that flows best is the order you finally have on your prompt card.
- Try to speak without looking at the prompt card.
- Look at your audience.

Decide on the age and character of the councillor you will be role playing at the council meeting. Take up that role from the moment you enter the classroom next lesson. You should stay in councillor role except when you are presenting your group's case.

Making your presentation

Aims

On these two pages you will:

- Make and evaluate your formal presentation.
- Take notes of the key points made at the meeting as the basis for a formal report.
- Reflect on your development as a speaker and identify areas for improvement.

Starter *as a class*

Special council meeting to discuss the future development of the Northfields site

Each group in turn should deliver their presentations. Remember to stay in councillor role except when you are presenting your group's case.

The leader of the council welcomes you to today's meeting.

In your role as a councillor you will:

- Evaluate the quality of the presentations
- Vote for the group that you judge to have made the most effective presentation
- Support your vote with evidence.

The leader of the council has provided you with an evaluation sheet. S/he will explain how you can use it to evaluate the debate.

In your role as a member of a group presenting a bid, you and your group will be called on to present your bid to the council in the order on the evaluation sheet.

> **! Remember**
>
> - Try to speak without looking at the prompt card.
> - Make eye-contact with the audience occasionally.
> - Speak clearly and vary the tone of your voice.
> - Don't speak too fast.

Introduction
as a class

Listen carefully while each group presents its case. Note the arguments used and how effectively each group presents those arguments.

Consider these questions especially:

- Does the introduction clearly put the audience in the picture?
- Is the order of the presentation logical?
- Is each person helping to illustrate the key points?
- Does the presentation end effectively?

Use the evaluation sheet (**Worksheet 105**) to summarize your points and award marks according to your evaluation.

Development
on your own

Complete your evaluation. Work out which group you wish to award the highest mark. Make certain that you can justify this: note your key reasons in the bottom section of the evaluation grid.

as a class

The leader of the council will hold the vote by saying the name of each bid in turn. Vote for the group you have awarded the most points. Once the meeting has made its decision, councillors who voted for the winning group will be asked to justify their decision.

Plenary

Write on your whiteboards three key elements that made the winning presentation so successful. See if there is agreement on deciding what these elements are.

homework

Fill in your drama evaluation record for homework, assessing your formal role playing as a bid presenter as well as how well you improvised the role of a councillor. Decide how you could have improved your contribution.

Planning a formal report

Aims

On these two pages you will:

- Think about ways of planning your report and use notes to aid this planning.
- Identify the different features of informal and formal English texts.
- Understand and explain what words mean in particular contexts.

Starter

In pairs, see if you can explain the precise meaning of the highlighted words in the context of the following sentences. In some cases it may be easier to think of an alternative word or phrase that would fit that context.

Be prepared to feed back your explanations or suggestions.

1. The girl hoped her school **report** would be lost in the post.
2. **Report** to me here at four o'clock.
3. Leonardo Da Vinci was a man of great **vision**.
4. The fog reduced **vision** to a few yards.
5. Genteel Victorian women were expected to be a **vision** of loveliness.
6. They requested a room with a **view**.
7. They had an appointment to **view** the house tomorrow.
8. The event had seemed very different from my point of **view**.
9. The **editorial** board meets every week.
10. The **editorial** condemned the Government's inaction.

Introduction in pairs

Today you will focus on how to plan your report of the council meeting that decided on the future of the Northfields School site. As always, before beginning any piece of writing the key things you have to consider are:

- **Purpose** and
- **Audience**

so that you can decide on the appropriate

- **Structure** and
- **Style.**

The *purpose* of the report is to provide a brief, unbiased, accurate record of the meeting. Its *audience* is council officials and anyone interested in the business of the meeting. But what about its *style*?

To help you understand the formal pattern of language that a formal report requires, you will be given 20 different sentence starters plus eight key-features cards, only half of which are suitable for a formal report (**Worksheet 106**). In pairs, sort the cards into two groups under the headings 'suitable for a formal report' and 'not suitable for a formal report'.

Be prepared to explain the reason for your selection.

Development as a class

Now it's time to plan the *structure* of this report. Look at the notes that you took at the council meeting and consider if they can help you plan your report.

Discuss with the person sitting next to you what structure you think this formal report should have, and use a whiteboard or piece of paper to write down the flow diagram that expresses this structure. Some of the formal sentence starters from the introduction activity may help you to think of sections that need to be included in your plan (see example below).

A meeting was held to discuss ...

↓

The first organization to present its bid was ...

↓

The main arguments supporting this bid were ...

↓

Be prepared to share your ideas with the rest of the class. See if the plan you suggested is similar to the plan the class collectively decides on.

All your preparations are now in place to begin your report. Next lesson you will be given around 30 minutes in which to write this report. Listen and watch carefully while your teacher models for you how to begin writing this sort of report, using the example below. Be prepared to join in the process.

Report of council meeting on the future of the Northfields site

The council meeting was called to provide a forum for groups wishing to present their bids for the development of the Northfields site ...

What would it be logical to cover next?

Plenary

On your whiteboard or a piece of paper jot down some key stylistic features of a formal report. See if the class is agreed on what these are, and if you can come up with an example of each.

Aims

On these two pages you will:

- Write your formal report within a fixed time limit.
- Check your work carefully and evaluate how its structure, style and handwriting could be improved.
- Identify the features of a text written in formal English.

Starter  as a group

Your teacher will read you a short extract from a formal report which was circulated to residents living in Brixton in London.

> **The Regeneration Game**
>
> In February, the Brixton Area Forum Board held a meeting to look at <u>regeneration</u>[1] and the consequences of <u>gentrification</u>[2] in Brixton. The invited speaker, Val Shawcross, Greater London Authority (GLA) member for the Brixton area, opened by describing the GLA's regeneration work and answered questions from the floor.
>
> A lively open discussion followed. Many issues were raised by participants, including the rapidly increasing rents in the area and the need to maintain a balance between big businesses and local enterprise ...

[1] *improving run-down and deprived areas – here used as a play on words echoing the TV programme 'The Generation Game'*
[2] *making run-down areas trendy and expensive*

In groups, annotate your copy of the text (**Worksheet 107**), identifying any features that relate to its structure or style, including how formal the language is. Be prepared to share your ideas with the class.

Introduction on your own

Your teacher will display the structure you agreed for your formal report (see page 123) and set you a time limit in which to complete it. Give it the title 'Report of council meeting on the future of the Northfields site'.

Follow these guidelines when writing your report:

- Keep your report as brief as possible, while ensuring that you cover the key points.
- Check that anybody reading your report who had not attended the meeting could understand it.
- Use your whiteboard or a piece of paper to help construct the more difficult sentences.
- Do not include any personal comment.
- Maintain third person, formal, impersonal English throughout.

Development on your own

Now you are going to evaluate your report using the sort of criteria an examiner would use. This is a difficult task, but essential if you are to learn to redraft your own work effectively.

Put yourself in the position of a reader of the report who has not attended the council meeting. Make certain that your report communicates the key points clearly. Fill in the evaluation grid on **Worksheet 108** to map out for yourself what you need to improve.

Plenary

Decide two or three things that you found most difficult about writing this report. Be prepared to share your ideas with the class.

Reviewing what's been learnt

In this section, you should have developed your ability to interpret playscripts as well as increased your understanding of how to make scripts effective. You should have developed your skills at improvising a role as well as devised a script to present that role. You have also taken part in a formal role play, both developing and presenting your ideas as part of a group and questioning ideas in role as a councillor.

Look through your drama record and decide on three key targets for you to improve.

> My targets to improve my role play and drama skills are:
> - _____
> - _____
> - _____

You have also written a formal report of a council meeting. What points do you think you need to focus on to improve your formal report writing skills? Decide on three targets.

> My targets to improve my formal report writing skills are:
> - _____
> - _____
> - _____

Pulling it all together

Introduction

Throughout Year 8, you have worked individually, in pairs and in small groups on developing your reading, writing and speaking and listening skills. In this section you are going to pull all these skills together to produce a class magazine which will showcase what you have learnt.

You will need to work together in groups to make decisions about the content and design of the magazine, and then research and write the articles. The magazine will contain a range of articles of different kinds, which will allow you to show how well you can write to persuade, inform, describe, argue and entertain. Your presentation and proofreading skills will be needed when you come to put the magazine together. Finally you will evaluate how successful the magazine is, and how well you have worked together to produce it.

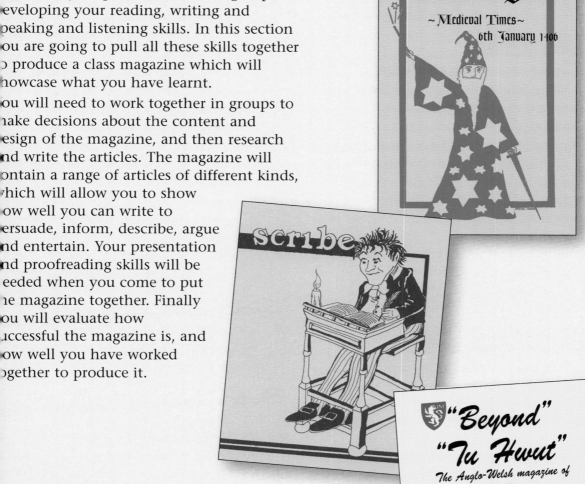

Key aim

In this section you will:

- Refine your writing and editing skills, working together to produce a class magazine.

Planning the contents

On these two pages you will:
- Consider the audience and content of the class magazine.
- Plan your own section as a group.

Starter `as a class`

In this section you are going to consolidate your groupwork and research and writing skills by producing a class magazine.

First of all, you need to consider the audience. Who are you writing this magazine for: all the members of the school community, including students, parents and teachers, or one specific group, such as other Year 8 students? Discuss your views on who the target audience for the magazine should be. How will this affect the content and style of the magazine?

Introduction `as a class`

Now you need to decide what you are going to include in the magazine. You are going to work in groups to produce articles that reflect the interests and activities of the class. These articles will be grouped together in sections on particular topics, such as:

- **Sports** – report on sports day, profiles of athletes in your class, feature on unusual or extreme sports …
- **Books** – top ten reads, short story, questionnaire on class/family reading habits …
- **Media** – feature on local cinemas, quiz on soaps, reviews of music, film and TV …

- **Fashion** – feature: what's in and what's out this year? comment: is fashion a waste of time? questionnaire: what do you wear? …
- **Consumer affairs** – questionnaire on mobile phone use, review of computer games, feature on local supermarkets …
- **Letters and advice** – problem page, horoscope, feature on teenage blues …
- **School issues** – readers' true experiences, feature on new bullying policy, profiles on staff members …

Your teacher will discuss all of these topic areas fully with you.

What's inside …

Sports
4 Sports day – full report
5 Top athletes in our midst…
6 Going to extremes

Books
7 Top ten reads
8 'The Visitor': a short story
10 What do you read?

Media
11 Going to a film?
12 How much do you know about soaps?
14 Reviews

Fashion
16 Beauty: 10 survival tips
17 What do you wear?
18 Is fashion a waste of time?

Development *as a group*

When you have decided on the overall contents of your magazine, you need to organize groups to work on the different topic areas. Your teacher will help you allocate people to the different groups.

Each group will be responsible for one topic area, covering two to four pages of the magazine. This section can include all sorts of different types of writing – reviews, information, imaginative writing, illustrations, questionnaires etc – but it must include a **feature article** on a particular topic. Every member of the group will write a feature article, and the best article will be included in the magazine.

Your first task as a group is to decide what **copy** you are going to write for the magazine. You will need to discuss this in some detail – use the grid on **Worksheet 109** to record all the articles you will be including and who will be responsible for writing each article. (You will fill in the third column on the grid in the next lesson.)

copy the written matter in a newspaper or magazine, as opposed to graphics or illustrations

feature article an article in a newspaper or magazine that covers a topic in an extensive and interesting way

---

! *Remember* to think about these issues when you are planning your section.

- As well as longer written articles, what else are you going to include in your section? For example, cartoons, illustrations, puzzles …

- What skills do you need to be able to complete your work? Make sure you use the talents of everyone in your group – at research or interviewing, illustration, ICT …

- Remember that each person in the group must write a feature article as well as other types of copy.

- Before you decide on the title of your feature article, think about where you are going to get your information from, such as questionnaires, interviews, books or the internet. Have you set yourself a realistic task?

Plenary

Feed back to the class the decisions you have made.

- What problems did you come up with?

- Has the class got any ideas to help you with these problems?

Interviews and questionnaires

Aims

On these two pages you will:

- Research the information that you need to write your articles.
- Consider what makes good questionnaires and interviews.

Starter  on your own

It is important for you to plan your work in detail before you start writing. For many articles, you will need to research background information, conduct interviews, hand out questionnaires and collect together material from different sources. Think about what you will need for your contribution to the magazine.

Make notes on what the tasks you have chosen involve, and add this to the final column of your grid on **Worksheet 109**. For example, if you were Jan, a member of the group compiling the sports section of the magazine, and you were writing profiles on class athletes and a feature on extreme sports, you would fill in your section of the grid like this:

Introduction as a group

You may find that you want to survey people's opinions as part of your research. Two good ways of doing this are by carrying out:

- Interviews
- Questionnaires.

Interviews are conducted orally, usually with a single person; the interviewer writes down or records the responses. Questionnaires are written documents which are filled in by a single respondant. They are useful when you want to find out similar information from lots of people, such as your classmates.

Whether you are conducting an interview or a questionnaire, it is important to remember who your audience is.

Look at the questionnaire on **Worksheet 11** It was planned as part of the research for a 'Top Ten Books' feature. In groups, discuss the following features of questionnaires, using the example provided to focus your thoughts. Consider the following questions:

1 Is it important to have a title?
2 Will respondants always want to give their names?
3 What does 'delete as applicable' mean? Why is it a useful feature?
4 What kind of questions are asked on the questionnaire? Do they require different kinds of answer?
5 In what different ways could you use the information on this questionnaire?

Article	Who is responsible	What this task involves
Sports profiles	Jan	Interview four of the best class athletes, and write this up in question and answer format. Include photos if room.
Feature on extreme sports	Jan	Research extreme sports on internet, and public library for info on local societies. Good pics needed.

in pairs

Now draft your own questionnaire to help you with the article that you are working on. Use the advice in the information box (right) to help you plan your questions.

Swap your questionnaire with a partner's and give constructive criticism. Refine your questionnaire in light of this feedback.

as a group

You may also want to interview one or more people as part of your research. In groups, think about what factors make a successful interview.

Consider the following issues:

- Arranging a time and place
- What you should take with you
- What kind of questions you should ask
- What listening skills are required
- What you should do at the end of the interview.

Fill in the grid on **Worksheet 111** with advice that you would give someone planning to conduct an interview. Be prepared to feed back your advice to the class. Add further points to your grid in light of the class discussion.

Development *on your own*

Spend the rest of the lesson researching your articles. When you have completed all your research, you need to collect your material together and decide what you are going to use in your copy. If you are not sure what to include, ask someone in your group to help you.

Asking the right questions

Successful interviews and questionnaires depend on the right questions being asked.

Closed questions are questions that require a 'yes' or 'no' answer, or an answer limited to a list of choices. They don't give you in-depth answers, but you can use them to check facts, and they are easy to analyse. For example:

- Did you enjoy this book?
- How often do you use a computer?
  - (a) every day ☐
  - (b) twice a week ☐
  - (c) once a week ☐
  - (d) less than once a week ☐

Open questions are questions designed to get as much information as possible. No choices are given, so people are free to answer in whichever way they like. For example:

- What do you think about the school's bullying policy?
- How would you describe your experience of …?

Probing questions can be used to follow up open questions. They invite your respondant to go deeper into an answer, so that you can find out more about a subject. Examples include:

- In what way?
- Will you expand on that please?
- Why is that important to you?

Plenary

Using your whiteboard or a piece of paper, jot down three things to remember about good questionnaires, and three things about good interviews.

Be prepared to feed back your points to the class.

homework

Complete your research for homework.

Writing feature articles

Aims

On these two pages you will:
- Consider the structure and style of feature articles.
- Write the first draft of your own feature article.

Starter  in pairs

You will all be writing a feature article as part of your section of the magazine. The best feature in each group will be included in the magazine when it is put together.

The key to good feature writing is its structure. In pairs, discuss why you think structure is so important when you are producing an extended piece of writing such as a feature.

Introduction as a class

The flowchart (right) shows you a good way of structuring your feature article. Read it through as a class.

Now read the feature 'The graffiti king makes good' on page 133. Discuss whether this feature follows the structure suggested in the flowchart. How effective is it as a result?

 as a group

Of course, other factors contribute to making features successful, including the language and style in which they are written. In groups, discuss what aspects of language and style you would focus on to write a good feature. Consider the following:
- Tone
- Register
- Narrative perspective
- Emotive language
- Powerful verbs and vivid adjectives
- Imagery.

Beginning
➤ An introduction that hooks the reader into the story (it need not say what the story is about).
➤ A key paragraph that states what the feature is about.

Middle
➤ Several paragraphs that contain the bulk of the story, plus any background and less important information.
➤ It should contain quotations, perhaps from your interview, that reveal emotion or character.
➤ This section can be structured with a beginning, a middle and an end of its own.

End
➤ A final paragraph that sums up the feature's argument or story.
➤ It may include an echo, idea or image from earlier in the story.

Development as a group

Now write the first draft of your feature article, writing your final version for homework.

> **!** **Remember** to read your work through carefully, correcting any errors and redrafting sentences that could be improved. Have you given your article an effective structure? Have you paid attention to the aspects highlighted in your group discussion as part of the introduction activity above? Finish with a brief comment summing up how well you think you have completed the task.

Plenary

Share some of the opening paragraphs of your draft feature articles and decide what makes them successful.

The graffiti king makes good

This month, artist Arron Bird's work will be on sale in thousands of supermarkets. He once painted on walls – now he's the designer of Sprite's new drink cans.

When Arron Bird came home from work the other day, he found his two-year-old son Kaine had scribbled all over the living-room wall. Most dads would have been cross, but Arron could only smile. After all, as Kaine said: 'Daddy draws on walls.' And it's true.

In fact, 29-year-old Arron's reckoned to be one of Britain's leading graffiti artists and his talent has won him a lucrative contract with soft drinks giant Coca-Cola – designing its new Sprite cans. This month, Arron's street style designs, in aquamarine and silver, are on sale nationwide and his solo exhibition called Minuteman has just opened in Birmingham.

'It's like winning the lottery,' admits Arron, whose love of spray-painting derelict walls began when he was 11 years old and totally frustrated by his failure at school.

'I never felt comfortable in class,' he remembers. 'No one realised I was dyslexic. I hated reading out loud, so I fooled around to detract attention from me. Of course, I got labelled as being disruptive.

'The only thing I was good at was drawing. Art lessons should have been good, but they were boring. Everything the teacher was teaching us, I could already do. At break, when we'd go outside, I used to lose my rag a bit and sound off to my mate. That's how I got my nickname of Temper.'

Looking for stimulation, Arron read about hip-hop culture and graffiti art in a magazine and was 'blown away'.

'My friend's dad worked in a car shop, so I asked him to get me a few spray cans,' says Arron. 'He came back with half a dozen. I'd already seen the perfect place, a dark, creepy wall covered in fungi in an underpass nearby. People hardly went there because it was so horrible. We got some torches, waited 'til dark and crept in. I suppose I knew it was illegal, but it didn't seem to register.'

'I scraped off the fungi with an old can and then started spraying bright yellow and red everywhere. It was brilliant. I covered an area about 12ft by 9ft in beautiful colours with a character in ski-goggles in the foreground. I wanted to add my signature, so I wrote

Temper, the name I still use today.'

Soon Temper creations were appearing overnight on crumbling walls all over his home town of Wolverhampton. 'I never thought of myself as a vandal,' says Arron. 'I always chose ugly, unwanted sites and made them beautiful. Often I painted over nasty slogans such as "National Front" and "Wogs Out" and replaced them with bright pictures. Designing with spray cans is difficult because aerosols aren't designed to draw with, but I learnt my craft as I went.'

Arron started demonstrating his art at festivals. At the 2000 Sprite Urban Games exhibition in London, Arron's image of a breakdancer caught the attention of Coca-Cola bosses, who asked him to submit designs for the new Sprite can. 'I sent them a handful of different sketches,' says Arron. 'But I heard nothing for eight weeks. Then, suddenly, they phoned to say I'd been chosen to design the can. It was a great break and now things are going so well, I know this is just the beginning.'

Linda Hawkins

Editorial decisions

Aims

On these two pages you will:

- Elect an editorial committee, which will make decisions on the overall look of the magazine.
- Finalize your own copy for the magazine.

Starter

Look at all the feature articles written by your group members and decide which works best. This article will be selected as your group's feature contribution to the class magazine.

Nominate the successful feature writer to join the editorial committee, which will make decisions about the overall look of the magazine. He or she will have to tell the committee what other copy their group is producing for the magazine, so you must decide this now as a group.

Introduction *as a group*

The editorial committee members will report back their decisions to the group at the end of the lesson. While they are making these decisions, the rest of the group members should continue to work on their copy.

The editorial committee will need to consider various issues (see panel, right).

You should make detailed notes about the decisions you make, so that you can feed back to your group all the relevant information. You should also give a copy of these notes to your teacher.

What are you going to call the magazine? Brainstorm a list of names together. You may need to get the opinion of the rest of the class by voting for the favourite title.

Decide on an image for the front cover. You should bear in mind your target audience when you do this.

Draw up a list of contents. Each committee member should bring details of what members of their group are writing. Decide how many pages should be allocated to each section, and use the page planner on **Worksheet 112** to plan the exact contents and order of your group's section of the magazine. Then decide on the order of the different sections in the magazine, and draw up a contents page.

Make important decisions about the design of the magazine. What size are your pages going to be? Will the pages be divided into columns? Are you going to use the same font all the way through? Or one font for all the feature articles, another for all the reviews etc? Will there be any other design features running through the magazine?

While the editorial group is making decisions about the magazine, you need to get to work on finalizing your copy. Use the skills that you have practised throughout the year. For example:

● **If you are writing a review** – remember to hook the reader in with your opening sentences, put the book (or film) in context and end with a statement summing up the effect of the book and giving its target audience. (See pages 92–93.)

● **If you are writing a short story** – think about your narrative perspective, how you can use vivid words and imagery, and whether you can create an atmosphere of tension, mystery or fear. (See pages 18–27.)

● **If you are writing an information or explanation text** – think about how formal your language should be, what tense and person you should use, and how the piece should be structured to suit its purpose, using connectives effectively. (See pages 40–59.)

Development as a group

When you have completed a rough draft of your work, get someone else in your group to read it.

● Can they spot any spelling mistakes?

● Is it effectively paragraphed?

● Could anything be added or taken away to improve it?

In addition, complete any illustrations, cartoons, puzzles or competitions etc that you will need on your pages.

Plenary

The editorial committee should report back to the groups on the decisions made. Make sure that you know how long your article should be, what design features should be included and how it should fit into the page layout of the magazine.

Write final drafts of your articles for homework, bearing in mind the decisions made by the editorial committee.

 Aims

On these two pages you will:
- Print out, check and assemble the class magazine.
- Evaluate how successful the magazine is.

Starter *on your own*

Each group member should print out their article, following the page layout agreed on by the editorial committee. (Anyone who hasn't composed their article on a word processor will have to key it in first, of course.)

- Make sure you save your work regularly – you don't want to lose it accidentally.
- Don't just rely on the spell-checker – you need to proofread the work yourself as well. Computers only pick up wrong spellings – they don't know whether you have used the right word.
- If you're using text boxes and picture boxes, make sure you've got enough room to fit your text and pictures in.

Introduction *as a group*

Now put all the pages of your section together and print out a first draft. Decide what needs to be cut or added so that it fits on the pages allocated (see box, 'Cutting text').

Scan your print-out for any obvious errors in spelling, punctuation and layout, then proofread it more carefully for anything you may have missed. Make sure your article is proofread by somebody else, as they

Cutting text

Magazine articles often need cutting so that the material fits neatly on the page.

This also applies to books: look at the extract on page 137, which is the first **proof** of one of the pages of this book. Can you see where the text has overrun the page area? This has been labelled 'overmatter'.

There are various ways of dealing with overmatter:
- ✂ Cut unimportant sentences or paragraphs
- ✂ Reword sentences so that they are more concise
- ✂ Cut whole articles if necessary
- ✂ Put articles on other pages of the publication where there is more room
- ✂ Cut photos or artwork.

Now look at page 21 in this book. How did the editors deal with the problem of overmatter?

proof a print-out for the correction of errors

are more likely to pick up errors than you are. (Often a writer will read what they think is on the page – or what they think makes sense – rather than what is actually there.) Check if:

- Capital letters are in the right place
- Punctuation is accurate, especially in direct speech
- The layout is effective, including headings and subheadings
- The illustrations are the right size and in the right place, and have appropriate captions.

Make any changes necessary on screen, then print out a final version. Your member of the editorial committee should take your printed section to a meeting to assemble the class magazine.

Development *as a class*

Look at the completed magazine and evaluate how successful you have been in completing the task and writing appropriately for your audience.

Plenary

Decide which three things you did best as a group in this project, and which three things caused the most problems.

Post–1914 novel

Introduction

When a writer starts to write, whether it is fiction or non-fiction, a novel, reportage or a poem, a number of decisions need to be made. One of the most important of these is choosing the **narrative perspective**. The narrative perspective provides the reader with a window through which the world created by the writer can be seen and experienced.

Sometimes an author will choose to tell a story through the 'voice' of one of the characters. This means that the character concerned tells the story directly, in the first person. Consequently the reader experiences everything from the point of view of that person alone.

as a class

Look again at the extract from *Heaven Eyes* above, and discuss these questions:
1. Who has the author chosen to be the narrator of the story?
2. How do we know this?
3. What are the advantages and disadvantages of telling a story in this way?

in pairs

In pairs, discuss these questions:
1. How do you think this particular narrative perspective will affect the reader? For example, will it give the reader greater understanding of feelings, or help to explain actions and events in an unbiased way?
2. In what way would the reader's understanding be different if the author had chosen a different narrative perspective, such as third-person narration?

narrative perspective the point of view from which a story is written

overmatter

Development *in pairs*

Read the extract from *Heaven Eyes* on **Worksheet 1.5**. In pairs:
1. Highlight all the first-person pronouns (I, me, my, we, us).
2. Rewrite the first paragraph, changing the narrative voice from first to third person (for example, 'my' becomes 'her', 'I' becomes 'she', etc.). You may also need to make a few other changes to other words in places (see the example below).
3. Discuss what difference this makes to your involvement in the story as a reader.
4. Which version do you think is more effective? Why?

Here's the first bit to start you off:

Erin asked herself if this was the scariest moment of her life. No, she thought, that was the moment when her mother closed her eyes for the final time and left her all alone.

Plenary

How do you know when an author is speaking to you, the reader, directly? Why do you think they might do this?

Why do authors comment on, or hint at, what is going to happen in the story?

What are the advantages and disadvantages of telling a story in the first person?

homework

Imagine a frightening or sad moment in your own life. Using the David Almond extract as a model, write an opening paragraph to your story which:
- Speaks to the reader directly.
- Comments on, or hints at, the story that will follow.

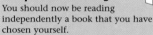

Independent reading

You should now be reading independently a book that you have chosen yourself.
- How does the author of your chosen book engage your interest as a reader?
- What narrative perspective has the author used?

Record your answers on **Worksheet 1.3**.

! **Remember** to read your work carefully, improve it if necessary, and write a brief comment on how well you think you have completed the task. Remember that you do not have to write the whole story – just the opening paragraph.

overmatter

Reviewing what's been learnt

In this section you have consolidated the skills you have been developing throughout Year 8 in reading, writing and speaking and listening work. Most importantly you have:

- Co-operated with other people, taking different roles in a group in order to plan and produce a magazine.
- Developed your research skills.
- Written your own copy, paying attention to the target audience for your work.
- Edited your work, and the work of other members of your group.
- Used your ICT skills to desk-top publish your magazine.

Think about your performance in this section. Did you:

- Contribute fully to group discussions?
- Research your articles using questionnaires and interviews?
- Work independently to write your copy?

Now it's time to think about what things you have learnt from this section, and list the key points in your exercise book, using the following sentence starters to help you:

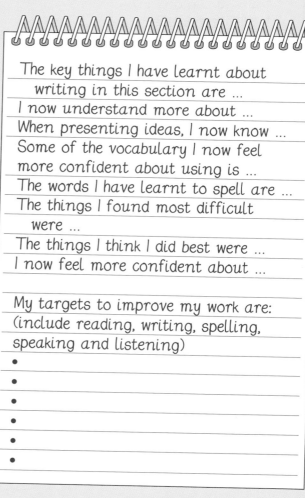

The key things I have learnt about writing in this section are ...

I now understand more about ...

When presenting ideas, I now know ...

Some of the vocabulary I now feel more confident about using is ...

The words I have learnt to spell are ...

The things I found most difficult were ...

The things I think I did best were ...

I now feel more confident about ...

My targets to improve my work are: (include reading, writing, spelling, speaking and listening)

-
-
-
-
-
-

Introduction

Doing tests and exams can seem very frightening, but if you prepare for them thoroughly, you should feel much more confident about them. You will have completed tests at the end of Year 6 and will have been given a National Curriculum level that reflected your progress in Maths, English and Science. You may have also done tests at the end of Year 7 to measure your progress since primary school, and to allow you to set targets for Year 8. Now you are in Year 8, you have another chance to show what you can do in some more tests. You will be able to see how much progress you have made, and what targets you need to set as you start Year 9.

This section guides you through the tests, explaining what you need to know so that you can show off your skills to their best advantage.

Key aims

In this section you will:

- Understand the assessment criteria for the reading and writing tests.
- Examine the types of question on reading and writing that you are given in the NC Tests and attempt sample tests to practise your skills.

MINOR TASK: *Review*

You should spend about 25 minutes on this task

Television Review – factual programmes

People are interested in TV documentaries.
They like finding out about other people, wildlife and faraway places.
Here are some of the reasons why people enjoy them:

> I'm really nosy – I like to find out about other people's lives.

> I enjoy seeing what happens to people in everyday situations – at the airport, in schools or in a hotel.

> I like finding out about how animals live in the wild.

> Documentaries help me with my schoolwork.

Write a review of any documentary or factual programme you have seen. Explain why you liked it and why others might enjoy it.

(20 marks)

PLANNING

A review should contain:

- a short summary of what it is about;
- your opinion – why you like it, and who else you think it should appeal to and why.

The following planning frame will help you organize your ideas for your review.

- Title

- Subject and focus of programme – main 'characters'

MAJOR TASK: *Science fact or fiction?*

You should spend about 40 minutes on this task

Time Travel!

You and a friend have discovered a mysterious machine which unexpectedly whisks you back in time.

Write a story exploring an adventure you have in the past.

PLANNING

You will need to decide:

- Story title

- Introduction – how are you going to grab your reader's attention?

- Characters – who are they? Describe them in outline

- Narrative voice – who is telling the story?

- Plot outline, including complication and crisis

- Resolution – how are you going to tie up the story, making sure there are no loose ends?

The reading test: fiction (1)

Aims

On these two pages you will:

- Be introduced to the Year 8 reading test.
- Explore the reading skills that will be assessed in the test.
- Examine the types of question on the fiction extract that require short answers.

Starter *in pairs*

The grid on **Worksheet 113** lists the 'assessment focuses' for the reading test – that is, they describe what the examiners will be assessing in your reading work.

1   In pairs, read these statements carefully and talk about them, making sure you know what they mean. Write down what you think they mean in the second column on the grid. For example, against 'Deduce, infer or interpret information, events or ideas' you might write:

   Read between the lines, to find out more about characters and events.

2   When you have explored the assessment criteria, decide on your own which you think you can do with confidence, and put a tick against those statements.

3   Now put a tick against those areas that you find most difficult: these are the ones you should target to help you prepare most effectively for the tests.

4   Discuss with your partner what you have done and see if you can help each other to think of ways in which you can meet your targets.

Be prepared to feed back your ideas to the class.

Introduction *as a class*

The Year 8 reading test is similar to the one you completed in Year 7. You will be given a booklet which contains different kinds of fiction and non-fiction texts. These texts will have an emphasis on science and technology. They will also have a linking theme, such as dinosaurs. As in Year 7, you will have 15 minutes at the start of the test to read the different extracts. You will then have 1 hour and 15 minutes to answer the questions in the answer booklet.

Each question will have a particular focus, testing a different aspect of your reading skills. You have already studied these assessment focuses in the starter activity. You may be asked to give one-word answers, to complete a table or to write longer answers of several sentences. Some questions will ask you to compare different texts.

There will be about 19 questions in the booklet, so you will need to make sure that you manage your time effectively. It is sensible to spend most time on the questions with most marks. If you can't find the answer to a question carrying only one mark, don't waste loads of time looking for it – go on to the next question, and come back to the question at the end of the test.

Your teacher will give you copies of a sample fiction text for a Year 8 reading test (**Worksheet 114**). This lesson you are going to focus on the questions requiring short answers. In the next lesson you will be looking at the questions that require longer answers.

Read this text carefully as a class, then discuss the following questions.

1. Complete the following table, listing three different things that have been noticed about the footprint. The first one has been done for you.

Quotation from text	What this tells you
1 'The enormous three-toed track'	it's printed in the mud
2.	
3.	

This question tests your ability to find information in the text, and to use quotations as evidence. It's only worth one mark, though, so don't spend too much time on it.

2. Why does Lord John Roxton think it is important that water is still dripping into the footprint? Tick one box.
There will be something for him to drink ☐
He can follow the animal ☐
It shows that the animal only passed through recently ☐
He will be able to shoot the animal ☐

(1 mark)

3. Look at the section 'Sure enough...' to 'a sight like that'. From this section, how do you know that Challenger is knowledgeable? Give **two** examples of what he says or does and explain how this shows he is knowledgeable.

(4 marks)

Both these questions are testing your ability to deduce or infer (work out) information from what is written in the passage. Not only have you got to find examples from the text – you've got to try to understand what the author is telling us about characters and events beyond the words on the page.

4. Look at the paragraph beginning 'There were, as I say...'. Why does the narrator describe the animals as *like monstrous kangaroos*?

(2 marks)

Your answer should make a comment on the writer's use of language, including any grammatical and literary features. Don't forget to use the term 'simile'.

Development *on your own*

Now answer all the questions on the extract on **Worksheet 115**.

> **! Remember**
> - To help you decide how much detail to give in an answer, look at the number of marks allocated to the question.
> - If you finish early, check your work.

Plenary

Feed back your answers to the questions.

What have you learnt about the types of question in the reading test that require short answers?

The reading test: fiction (2)

Aims

On these two pages you will:

- Examine the types of question on the fiction extract that require longer answers.
- Practise your skills in using quotations and formal language in your answers.
- Remind yourself of the features of certain text types.

Starter  in pairs

You will read a range of text types as part of your reading test. You have already read an example of narrative writing, and you are also going to read examples of discursive and explanation texts.

In pairs, fill in the grid on **Worksheet 116** to remind you of the features of these text types.

Introduction as a class

This lesson you are going to look at the kind of questions in the reading test that require longer answers. You should give these more time, as they are generally awarded more marks.

Look at the next question on the fiction extract on **Worksheet 114**:

5. How does the writer build atmosphere and excitement in this text? You should write about:
- the dialogue;
- how the reader is led up to the discovery of the dinosaurs;
- the reactions of the narrator and the other characters to events.

(5 marks)

The question is asking you to comment on the structure and organization of the text, and how the various aspects, including dialogue and characterization, combine to create a particular effect on the reader.

In your answer you would need to cover the pointers listed in the bullet points, but make sure that you answer the main question, 'How does the writer build atmosphere and excitement in this text?'

Marks will be awarded if you use quotations or specific and detailed references to the text. Read through the extract again, underlining any words and phrases that you think you would include in your answer to this question. Use a different colour pen for each bullet point.

Flex your PECs!

Using quotations can seem difficult, but it's much easier if you remember to Flex your PECs:

- Point – first make your **point**.
- Evidence – then back it up with **evidence** quoted from the text.
- Comment – finally make a **comment** about the quotation which relates it to your main point.

This mnemonic will help you remember how to use quotations from a text in your answer. For example:

poi

Atmosphere is created in the text through the use of similes to describe the animals: 'the babies big as elephants', 'like monstrous kangaroos' and 'skins like black crocodiles'. evid effect of these comparisons is to emphasize the size of the creatures, and also to make them com sound slightly menacing and frightening.

Have a go at flexing your PECs!

Development in pairs

As well as using quotations, you also need to use the right kind of formal language in your answer to this question. There are many different linking words and phrases that can help you make your comments effectively. Some of these are listed below.

which suggests

gives the impression that

implies

indicates

increases the atmosphere by

creates a mood of

illustrates

evokes a feeling of

emphasizes

In pairs, fill in the grid on **Worksheet 117** by making a comment relating each quotation to the main point. Try to use one of the formal words or phrases in the list above in your comment, for example:

Point	Evidence	Comment
Lord John Roxton expresses great enthusiasm	'By George, this must be the trail of the father of all birds!'	Lord John's exclamation <u>emphasizes</u> how excited he is at the discovery

on your own

Now have a go at answering question 5 yourself in paragraph form:

5. How does the writer build atmosphere and excitement in this text? You should write about:
- the dialogue;
- how the reader is led up to the discovery of the dinosaurs;
- the reactions of the narrator and the other characters to events.

(5 marks)

Plenary

Share three things you need to remember when you are tackling the questions in the reading test that require longer answers.

The reading test: non-fiction

Aims

On these two pages you will:

- Examine the types of non-fiction extracts that you will get in the reading test.
- Answer a set of sample questions on dinosaurs.
- Develop your ability to work out the meaning of unknown words.

Starter on your own

Read the extract 'Iguanodon: perhaps the most successful dinosaur' (**Worksheet 118**). Underline any words that you don't understand, and make a list of them. Divide your list into:

- Nouns – words that you recognize as the names of things.
- Words that you don't understand but can work out from the context or from your knowledge of prefixes – for example, 'bipedally'. Write your own definitions for these words.
- Words that you need to look up in a dictionary.

Be prepared to share your lists with the class.

Introduction in pairs

In this lesson you are going to focus on the non-fiction texts which form part of your sample reading test. The questions on these texts are similar to those you answered on the fiction text: they require both short and longer answers, and each question focuses on a particular reading skill.

Some questions ask you to comment on how the presentational or language features of the extract contribute to its meaning. In pairs, try to answer the following questions on the extract on **Worksheet 118**. Use the guidance points beneath the questions to help you answer them.

6. Subheadings are used in the extract at the beginning of paragraphs: *How did Iguanodon walk?* and *What preyed on Iguanodon?* Why do you think the writer has decided to use subheadings?

(2 marks

This question is aimed at encouraging you to think about the structure of the extract – what do these subheadings add to the text?

7. In the paragraph that begins '*Like many living herbivores*', what is the effect of using adjectives like *aggressive* and verbs and verb participles like *attacked*, *fall prey to* and *scavenging*?

(1 mark)

This question is asking you to comment on the effect of these words on the reader: what do they emphasize?

8. This extract is taken from a book accompanying a TV series. It contains quite a lot o difficult vocabulary that you may have to guess th meaning of from the context. Give the meaning of the following words, and explain how you worked it out.
- bipedally
- herbivore

(1 mark each

Look back at the starter activity. Remember to use the context, or your knowledge of prefixes or etymology, to help you.

Development on your own

You will also have to answer questions on the text as a whole, considering the writer's purpose and the overall effect of the text on the reader.

Write your answer to the following questions on your whiteboard, or on a piece of paper, before sharing them with the class.

9. One purpose of this text is to provide a scientific context for the TV programme *Walking with Dinosaurs*. We can tell this because the programme is mentioned in the opening sentence.
Find examples of two more ways that you can tell that this is a purpose of the text.
(2 marks)

10. What evidence is there in the text to support the claim of the title that Iguanodon is *perhaps the most successful dinosaur*? Is this an effective title?
(3 marks)

Plenary

Discuss key points to remember when doing the Year 8 reading test.

homework

Your teacher will give you a copy of the text 'Recreating dinosaurs – fact or fiction?' and a set of test questions to accompany it (**Worksheets 119, 120**). Read the text and complete the questions for homework. Remember to think carefully about what the question is asking you to do before you write your answer.

The writing test: minor task

Aims

On these two pages you will:

- Be introduced to the Year 8 writing test.
- Explore the assessment criteria for writing in the National Curriculum, and the writing skills that will be assessed in the test.
- Attempt a minor writing task.

Starter as a group

Your teacher will give you a number of different statements which describe achievement at levels 5 and 6 in writing in the National Curriculum (**Worksheet 121**).

1   In groups, read through the statements together and talk about what you think they mean.

2   Sort them into piles: which ones describe level 5, and which ones describe the higher level 6?

3   Discuss your views with the rest of the class, and rearrange your piles if necessary.

4   Discuss in your groups what skills someone would need to show in their writing in order to jump from level 5 to level 6. Can you set yourself a target in the light of this discussion?

Be prepared to feed back the targets that you set.

Introduction

You have completed many writing tasks throughout the year in English, adapting your style for different purposes and audiences. The Year 8 writing test concentrates on writing to *explore, imagine, entertain,* and writing to *analyse, review, comment.* It consists of a major task, which is a longer piece of writing, and a minor task which is more specific and requires more concise answers. The test lasts for 1 hour and 15 minutes; you will need to spend about 40 minutes on the major task and 25 minutes on the minor task, and you should aim to give yourself about 10 minutes to plan and check your work

This lesson you are going to attempt the kind of writing test that might be given to you as your minor task. The following skill areas are assessed in the minor task:

- **Vocabulary** (4 marks). Marks are awarded for the selection and use of a range of words for precision and effect.

- **Sentence structure/punctuation and paragraph organization** (8 marks). This includes the way in which sentences are organized within paragraphs, using a variety of phrases and clauses, appropriate connectives and the correct punctuation.

- **Composition and effect** (8 marks). Marks are awarded for imaginative writing which appeals to the reader and is appropriate to its purpose.

in pairs

Read the sample minor task below. Working in pairs, discuss the following questions before you start to write:

- What is the purpose of this piece of writing?
- Who is your intended audience?
- What register of language should you use?
- How can you show off your writing skills and vocabulary in this activity?

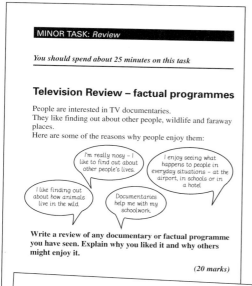

MINOR TASK: *Review*

You should spend about 25 minutes on this task

Television Review – factual programmes

People are interested in TV documentaries.
They like finding out about other people, wildlife and faraway places.
Here are some of the reasons why people enjoy them:

I'm really nosy – I like to find out about other people's lives.

I enjoy seeing what happens to people in everyday situations – at the airport, in schools or in a hotel.

I like finding out about how animals live in the wild.

Documentaries help me with my schoolwork.

Write a review of any documentary or factual programme you have seen. Explain why you liked it and why others might enjoy it.

(20 marks)

PLANNING

A review should contain:

- a short summary of what it is about;
- your opinion – why you like it, and who else you think it should appeal to and why.

The following planning frame will help you organize your ideas for your review.

- Title

- Subject and focus of programme – main 'characters'

- Setting

- Narrator

- What I liked about it

- Who else might enjoy it and why

Remember that you do not need to write more than four paragraphs.

Development *on your own*

Working on your own, use the planning sheet to plan your writing (**Worksheet 122**). Don't spend more than 5 minutes on planning. Then spend 25 minutes writing your review.

! Remember

- The planning sheet will not be marked – it is there to help you do your best work in the test.
- Pay attention to your sentence structure, punctuation and paragraph organization.
- Think about the impact of your writing, and be clear about its audience and purpose.
- Show that you have a wide range of vocabulary and always look for the right word to use.

Plenary

- What have you learnt about the minor writing task?
- What must you do to make sure you are successful?

The writing test: major task

Aims

On these two pages you will:

- Consider the skill areas that will be assessed in the major task.
- Attempt a major writing task.
- Practise applying your knowledge of spelling rules and patterns.

Starter

This lesson you are going to attempt a major writing task. One of the skill areas assessed in the major task is spelling. Your teacher is going to test you on 20 words that students in your class have had difficulty spelling this year. After this test, add any words that you have had difficulty spelling to your spelling log.

Introduction

The following skill areas are assessed in the major task:

- **Sentence structure and punctuation** (5 marks). Students are awarded high marks if they use correctly a range of sentence structures related to the demands of the task.
- **Paragraph organization and textual cohesion** (5 marks). This includes the way that sentences are organized within paragraphs as well as the overall organization of the writing.
- **Composition and effect** (15 marks). Marks are awarded for imaginative writing which appeals to the reader and is appropriate to its purpose.

Note that this comprises half the marks available for the major task.

- **Spelling** (5 marks). Note that more marks are awarded for attempting to spell difficult words than for the correct spelling of straightforward words.

in pairs

Read the sample major task below. Working in pairs, discuss the following questions before you start to write:

- Who is the target audience for this piece of writing?
- What type of language should I include to interest them?
- What writing skills do I need to draw on – description, direct speech …?

MAJOR TASK: Science fact or fiction?

You should spend about 40 minutes on this task

Time Travel!

You and a friend have discovered a mysterious machine which unexpectedly whisks you back in time.

Write a story exploring an adventure you have in the past.

Remember that stories usually include:

- an exciting opening to grab the reader's attention;
- a plot to keep them interested;
- paragraphs giving details of a crisis and complication;
- a conclusion providing resolution.

(30 marks)

Working on your own, use the planning sheet to plan your writing (**Worksheet 123**). Don't spend more than 5 minutes planning, but use your time wisely – you may like to try out one or two ideas to see which works best. (The planning sheet will not be marked – it is there to help you do your best work in the test.)

PLANNING

You will need to decide:

- Story title
- Introduction – how are you going to grab your reader's attention?
- Characters – who are they? Describe them in outline
- Narrative voice – who is telling the story?
- Plot outline, including complication and crisis
- Resolution – how are you going to tie up the story, making sure there are no loose ends?

Development

Write the introduction to your story and swap it with a partner's. Can they give you any advice on how to improve it?

> **! Remember**
>
> - Composition and effect count for half of your marks. Think about the impact of your writing, and be clear about its audience and purpose.
> - Pay attention to your sentence structure and paragraph organization.
> - Use spelling rules to help you with your spelling, and if you can't remember how to spell a word then have a guess. You will be rewarded for attempting to spell difficult words.
> - Check your work carefully when you have finished.

Plenary

- What have you learnt about the major writing task?
- What must you do to make sure you are successful?

Complete the writing task for homework, giving yourself about 35 minutes to finish it.

149

Reviewing what's been learnt

In this section you will have gained a better understanding of the skills that you need to acquire in order to be successful in the Year 8 optional tests. In particular you have:

- Explored the skill areas that are assessed in the reading and writing tests.
- Examined the types of question that are asked in the tests, and practised these tasks.

Reflect on your performance in the sample reading test and identify areas that you need to work on. Think about how well you can:

- Describe, select or retrieve information, events or ideas from texts and use quotation and reference to text
- Deduce, infer or interpret information, events or ideas from texts
- Comment on the structure and organization of texts, including grammatical and presentational features
- Comment on the writers' uses of language, including grammatical and literary features
- Identify and comment on the writers' purposes and viewpoints, and the effect of the texts on the reader.

My targets to improve my reading skills are:

-
-
-
-
-

Now reflect on your performance in the sample writing test and identify areas that you need to work on. Think about these aspects of your writing skills:

- Sentence structure and punctuation
- Paragraph organization and textual cohesion
- Composition and effect
- Spelling
- Vocabulary.

My targets to improve my writing skills are:

-
-
-
-
-

Glossary

abbreviation a shortened version of a word or group of words. Common abbreviations include 'Mr' (for 'Mister'), Co. (for 'Company') and USA (for 'United States of America'). You can also use your own abbreviations to save space or time when writing notes or diaries.

abstract based on thoughts and ideas rather than physical objects; compare **concrete**

accent the way in which words are pronounced. Accent is determined by where people live, where they were born, their education and social class. Compare **dialect**.

acknowledgement a formal note of the source of a piece of information or of a quotation in a text. Acknowledgements include, as a minimum, the title and author of the text used.

active the 'voice' used when the subject of a sentence performs the action of the verb: 'The police arrested the man.' Compare **passive**.

adjective a word that describes something: 'the tall cupboard', 'the round balloon'

adverb a word or phrase that tells you more about a verb, an adjective or even a whole sentence: 'Leon spoke quietly', 'The brightly coloured shawl', 'I will give it to you tomorrow'

adverbial phrase a group of words that functions in the same way as an adverb: 'by car', 'a few days ago', 'of course', 'in a strange way'

advertisement a text advertising goods or services, especially in newspapers, magazines, television and radio

advice text that advises; words – either spoken or written – that give information or suggestions for how someone should act or behave

advise to offer information and suggestions for how someone should act or behave in a particular situation

agreement having the same opinion about a subject

alliteration the effect created when words next to or close to each other begin with the same letter or sound: 'several silent slithering snakes'

amendment alteration, change, improvement

analyse to look at something in detail as a way of understanding it better

analysis grid a grid which helps you to analyse a text by focusing on the different parts of it

anecdote a short, entertaining story about a person or event

annotate mark up with your own notes, which are usually made in the margin

antonym a word opposite in meaning to another word: 'good' and 'bad' are antonyms. Compare **synonym**.

apostrophe a punctuation mark used to indicate either possession (Tim's book) or omitted letters (can't)

argue to put forward a viewpoint

assessment a formal **evaluation**

assessment focus an aspect of reading or writing that is assessed by an examiner

assonance the effect created by the repetition of vowel sounds: 'green fields'

assumption a belief that something is true, without thinking about it

attainment target a list of the knowledge, skills and understanding that you need to achieve in each subject skill at every level. In English there are three attainment targets, one for each of the special skills: 1 speaking and listening, 2 reading and 3 writing.

audience the group of people watching or listening to a performance, especially of a play or concert; also, people who read or listen to any texts, whether newspapers, television programmes, books or films

aural to do with listening skills; compare **oral**

autobiography an account of a person's life told by themselves; compare **biography**

auxiliary verb a verb such as 'be', 'have' and 'do' which helps in the formation of tenses or questions

balanced not taking sides; a balanced analysis presents information factually without trying to bias the reader towards any viewpoint

ballad see **narrative poem**

biased unfairly presented to favour one point of view over another; see also **subjective**

bibliography the section of a text that lists further reading or acknowledges the sources used

biography an account of a person's life told by someone else; compare **autobiography**

blank verse verse that doesn't rhyme. It often has a regular pattern of ten syllables with five stresses in each line: 'For he to-day that sheds his blood with me'.

broadsheet a larger format newspaper; compare **tabloid**

brochure a booklet that gives information about a product or service

cartoon a drawing or series of drawings which are funny or make a point

CD-ROM a disk used with a computer system which can contain written information, moving and still images and sound

chairperson the person in charge of a debate, who decides when each person may speak

character a person in a novel, short story or play

characterization how characters are described or portrayed by the writer

chronological arranged in the order in which things happened

classification a broad descriptive statement about something. Information texts often begin with a classification: 'Primates are the higher mammals'.

classified advert a small **advertisement**, usually placed in a newspaper by individuals; they are usually arranged in categories (such as 'Situations Vacant') and set out in columns

clause the building block of a sentence; each clause must include a verb and normally includes a subject as well. Some sentences consist of a single clause: 'It was snowing.' Other sentences consist of two or more clauses: 'It was snowing and we were cold.' See also **subordinate clause**.

cliché a phrase or idea that has been used so much that it is no longer effective: 'explore every avenue', 'money doesn't grow on trees'

cliffhanger a situation that keeps the audience guessing what will happen in the next episode of a drama or story

clipped form a word formed from the reduction of another word: 'phone' from 'telephone'

closed question a question that requires a 'yes' or 'no' answer, or an answer limited to a list of choices; compare **open question**

coherence the underlying logic and consistency of a text. In a coherent text the ideas expressed should be relevant to one another so that the reader can follow the meaning.

cohesion the way in which the parts of a text fit together. This is often signposted by grammatical features such as **connectives**.

colloquial to do with conversation. Colloquial language is used in familiar, informal contexts.

comment to express a view on something based on an analysis of it

commentary an explanatory series of notes or comments

commercial a television or radio **advertisement**

comparison using different forms of adjectives and adverbs to compare things. When you compare two things or people you add the suffix 'er' or the word 'more': 'Mike was faster, but Lisa was more graceful.' When you compare more than two

things or people you add the suffix 'est' or the word 'most': 'It's the nicest house, but also the most expensive.'

complex sentence a sentence containing one main clause and one or more subordinate clauses

complication a problem which adds interest to the plot of a story

compound sentence a sentence made up of two or more main clauses joined by a conjunction such as 'and' or 'but': 'Richard went to the cinema but Ruth went bowling'

conclusion the summing up of an argument, placed at the end of the discussion or discursive text; in general, the end of a process

concrete based on physical objects rather than abstract ideas; compare **abstract**

concrete poem see **shape poem**

conjunction a word that joins parts of sentences: 'and', 'but', 'if', 'although', 'as', 'where'; see also **subordinating conjunction**

connective a word or phrase that links clauses or sentences and signals in which direction the ideas in the sentences are moving. Connectives can indicate, among other things, addition ('also', 'furthermore'), opposition ('however,' 'on the other hand'), reinforcement ('besides', 'after all'), explanation ('for example', 'in other words'), lists ('first', 'finally'), result ('therefore') and time ('meanwhile', 'later').

consonant any letter other than the **vowels**

content the substance of a text, as opposed to its form or style

context the parts of a text immediately before and after the part focused on, which make its precise meaning clear; looking at the context (that is, the rest of the sentence or passage) can often help you work out the meaning of a difficult word. Context is also the background to a text, which may include the effect of the place and time in which the author lived.

contraction the shortening of a word or words: 'she'll' is a contraction of 'she will'. When a word is contracted we use an **apostrophe** to indicate the omitted letters.

copy the written matter in a newspaper or magazine, as opposed to graphics or illustrations

crisis the critical point, or climax, of a story, which the plot has been building up to

criteria standards by which a piece of work is judged and graded

critical reader someone who reads a text in an active and critical way, searching for meaning and looking at what is both good and bad

cursive joined up (handwriting)

debate a formal discussion in which opposing views are expressed and a vote is taken at the end

description an account or picture of something in words. Descriptions are written in the present tense, and although they must be clear they can use powerful adjectives and verbs to make the description vivid and effective.

device a trick or a technique used by a writer to create a particular effect; see also **narrative device**

dialect a variety of English, often based on region, which has distinctive grammar and vocabulary. Compare **accent**.

dialogue a conversation between two people, which may be spoken or written. Dialogue can refer to the words that the characters speak in a play.

director the person in charge of a production of a play or film. The director is concerned not only with how the words should be spoken and how the characters move and act, but also with how the costumes, lighting and scenery contribute to the overall purpose and effect of the play.

direct speech a way of writing down speech which uses the actual words spoken, e.g. '"I'm tired," said Dave.' Compare **indirect speech**.

discursive text a text that presents argument and information from differing viewpoints. Discursive texts usually use the present tense and logical connectives and make clear the viewpoint expressed at every stage.

display advert an advertisement for a product, often with photographs and graphics, which is placed in a newspaper or magazine by a business

draft to produce an early version of a piece of written work. A text can be developed through a number of drafts before reaching its final version; this drafting process allows improvements and additions to be made and mistakes to be corrected.

drama a performance, or the type of literature intended for performance. Drama is associated not only with the theatre, but also with television, radio and film.

dramatic technique a way of making a playscript dramatic or exciting, such as adding a moment of tension, or creating a change of mood or pace

editorial an article in a newspaper which gives the opinion of the editor

elegy a sad poem or song about someone who has died

emotive designed to create emotion in the audience

entertain to keep someone or an audience interested or amused. Good fiction, for example, uses a variety of narrative devices to entertain its readers.

epitaph the words inscribed on a tombstone

etymological dictionary a dictionary that explains the origins of words

etymology an account of the origins and development of words; also, the derivation of a particular word

evaluate to weigh up how useful something is in the light of the task being set; also, an examination term which requires you to write about the strengths and weaknesses of a subject

evaluation an assessment of the strengths and weaknesses of something

evaluation grid a grid which helps you to evaluate something, for example a text or performance, by analysing its different parts or features

evidence information stated in support of a particular claim or argument; in general, anything that you see, read or are told that gives you reason to believe something

explanation text a text written to explain how or why something happens or is the case. Explanation texts develop ideas logically, use clear, descriptive writing and connectives expressing cause and effect, and are written in impersonal language in the present tense.

explore to investigate thoroughly. An explorer is someone who travels into undiscovered territory to find out more about it.

expression showing your ideas or feelings through your words, tone, gestures or actions

fable a traditional tale, often involving the supernatural, whose purpose is to convey a moral lesson

fact a piece of information which is true; compare **opinion**

factual based on facts and information rather than opinions and assumptions

farce a humorous play or scenario in which ridiculous and unlikely situations occur

feature article an article in a newspaper or magazine that covers a topic in an extensive and interesting way

fiction literature, especially novels and stories, that describes imaginary events and people. Sometimes, however, the setting may be a real place, or the story may be based on a real character or historical event.

figurative language the use of words or expressions in an abstract or imaginative way to create a particular impression or mood. Imagery such as **metaphors**, **similes** and **personification** are examples of figurative language

first person a way of describing a text in which the writer or speaker refers to himself or herself by using the pronouns 'I' and 'we'; compare **second person**, **third person**

font a style of printing type

formal language language that pays careful attention to Standard English. Formal language may make use of specialist terms and contain many sentences in the passive; it generally avoids slang, colloquialisms and contractions. Compare **informal language**.

free verse verse that has neither rhyme nor a regular rhythm

freeze frame an important moment in a play captured like a photograph to underline its significance

gender a way of categorizing nouns by the sex of the thing referred to, i.e. as masculine, feminine or neuter

genre term used to refer to different **text types**, such as narrative, recount and explanation. Genre also means a kind or style of art or literature, which has its own specific features. Comedy, tragedy and satire are genres of drama; genres of novels include horror, romance and science fiction. Genre can also refer to categories of writing, such as poetry, novels and drama.

glossary an alphabetical list of specialist terms with their definitions

grammar the rules of a language, which describe how words can be combined to form phrases, clauses and sentences

haiku a Japanese form of poetry. Haikus usually have three lines with 17 syllables in the pattern 5, 7, 5.

headword a word forming the heading of an entry in a dictionary or encyclopaedia. The headword of the next entry, for example, is 'helper verb'.

helper verb see **auxiliary verb**

home page the opening page of a **website**

homophone a word that sounds the same as another but has a different spelling and meaning: 'right' and 'write'

hypertext multimedia; a type of text that can form links to other texts

identify to name something

imagery the use of language to create a vivid image or picture. **Metaphor**, **simile** and **personification** are forms of imagery.

imagine to form a picture in your mind of something. Using your imagination can help you to understand what it would be like to be someone or somewhere else

imperative a sentence or clause that gives an instruction: 'Sit down', 'Cut the bread'

impersonal writing that uses the third person (he, she or it) is described as impersonal; 'I' is not used

improvise to compose a scene with little planning, or as you perform it

index an alphabetical list of items, usually found at the back of a book

direct speech (also known as reported speech) a way of writing down speech where the words are referred to indirectly: 'Dave said he was tired.' Compare direct speech.

formal language language that includes colloquial language, slang and the use of contracted forms of words: 'Don't you eat no poison berries.' Compare formal language.

formation text a text written to inform. Information texts use the present tense and the third person, make clear how the information is organized and linked, and often incorporate examples.

struction text a text written to help readers achieve certain goals, especially how to make or do something. Instruction texts generally include a statement of the goal ('How to make a sponge cake') and follow a sequence of steps in chronological order to achieve the goal ('Then cream the sugar and butter'). Imperative verbs are used, and connectives often refer to the order in which the various steps are to be taken ('First...', 'Next...').

teractive responding to the input of the user

terpret to present a piece of writing or music so that a particular meaning is given to it

troduction the opening section of a text which sets the scene or explains what is to follow

verted comma a punctuation mark used to show the beginning and end of direct speech or to highlight a

particular word ('Look out!' said Dave) (the word 'genuine'). Inverted commas are also known as quotation marks.

irony a type of humour in which words are used to imply the opposite of what they normally mean

jingle a short catchy phrase or rhyme set to music and used to advertise something on radio or television

key sentence the most important sentence in a paragraph

Key Stage 3 the term given to the first three years of secondary school in England, Wales and Northern Ireland

KWL grid a grid to structure your research thinking for a research project, which asks you what you already Know, what you Want to know, and what you have Learnt at the end of the project

Latin the language of the Romans, which provides the roots for thousands of English words and place names

layout the way a text is presented on the page

lead article the main article on a newspaper or magazine page

lead character the main character in a story or play

lead item the main item that begins a television or radio news programme

lead story the main plot, especially in a soap opera; also, the lead article

limerick a five-line comic verse made famous by a writer called Edward Lear. The first, second and fifth lines of a limerick are long, and the third and fourth lines are short; it follows the rhyming scheme a a b b a.

literacy reading and writing skill

literary non-fiction text based on real events in people's lives, such as biographies, autobiographies, diaries and letters

logical following a reasonable, well thought out, step-by-step approach, where the connections between each step are made clear

lyric poem a poem that focuses on an important moment in the poet's life, and is concerned with the emotions evoked by that event

magic e a spelling rule: if you add an 'e' onto a consonant-vowel-consonant (CVC) word, such as 'fat', the short vowel sound is turned into the long vowel sound ('fate'). In other words, adding 'e' to CVC words makes the vowel say its own name. The same is true of CCVC words, such as 'plan'.

masthead the title of a newspaper and accompanying logos that identify it

memoir an autobiographical record

metaphor a form of imagery when one thing is said to be another: 'You are my sun and my moon'

metre the way in which words and syllables are arranged in poetry or music to create a regular rhythm

mnemonic a strategy or method of remembering something: 'There is a rat in separate'

modal verb a type of auxiliary (or 'helper') verb which expresses possibility (can, might), speculation (could, might), permission (can, may), obligation (ought, should) or necessity (should, must)

monologue a speech made directly to the audience which reveals a character's inner thoughts

moral a short moral lesson at the end of a **fable**

morphology the consistent patterns of letters that make up words

myth an ancient story of gods or heroes which attempts to explain events or human nature

narrative a text which retells events, often in chronological sequence. Narrative texts may be fictional or non-fiction.

narrative device a trick used by an author to make their writing interesting and entertaining, such as the use of imagery, repetition and descriptive language

narrative perspective the point of view from which a story is written; compare **narrative voice**

narrative poem a poem that tells a story. Earlier narrative poems, called ballads, have short, regular verses with a rhyme scheme

narrative voice the 'person' that a writer uses to narrate a story: the two main narrative voices are **first person** (using 'I' and 'me') and **third person** (using 'he/she'); compare **narrative perspective**

navigable structured so that you can find your way around the text easily

NC level National Curriculum level – a grade between 1 and 8 which is given to your work

NCT National Curriculum Test. All students in England and Wales are expected to take NCTs in English, maths and science in Years 2, 6 and 9.

neutral see **unbiased**

non-fiction any form of text that is not **fiction**

non-Standard English written or spoken language that is informal or in a dialect; compare **Standard English**

noun a word that names an object or quality: 'dog', 'luck', 'Birmingham'

noun phrase a wider term than 'noun'. It often refers to a group of words in a sentence that functions in the same way as a noun: 'all the colours of the rainbow'. It can also refer to a single noun or pronoun.

object the person or thing being acted upon in a sentence: 'Winston scored a goal', 'We visited the Millennium Dome.' Compare **subject**.

objective based on fact and reason, unbiased, not influenced by personal feelings; compare **subjective**

OHP overhead projector

OHT a transparency used to display text on an overhead projector

omniscient author a narrative voice in which an author writes from the godlike perspective of knowing everything about the characters' innermost thoughts and feelings as well as all the events of the story

onomatopoeia the effect created by words which copy the sounds associated with their meaning: 'crack', 'hiss', 'murmur', 'quack'

open question a question designed to get as much information as possible; compare **closed question**

opinion a belief or view about something or someone; compare **fact**

opinion piece an article in a newspaper which presents a personal view on an important issue

oral to do with speaking rather than writing; compare **aural**

oral tradition the way in which traditional stories are handed down from one generation to the next by word of mouth; such stories are not written down until later

overmatter copy that has been typeset but that cannot be used for printing owing to lack of space

paragraph a section of a piece of writing, used to organize the argument or help readers follow the storyline. A new paragraph should mark a new topic or a change of focus; in dialogue paragraphs mark a change of speaker.

participle a form of the verb that can help to form a clause. Present participles are formed by adding '-ing' to the base form of regular verbs: 'needing', 'helping'. Past participles are formed by adding '-ed' to the base form of regular verbs: 'needed', 'helped'; many are irregular and have other endings: 'flown', 'kept', 'written'.

passive the 'voice' used when the subject of a sentence is acted upon by the verb: 'The man was arrested.' Passive sentences tell you what happened and who it happened to but they do not usually tell you who or what performed the action. Compare 'The man was arrested' (passive) with 'The police arrested the man' (**active**).

performance a live entertainment provided for an audience